CHRISTMAS PAST

Map of Christmas Land
Vintage postcard
ca. 1920

CHRISTMAS PAST

By Barbara Hallman Kissinger

Vintage postcard
Printed in Germany
ca. 1912

PELICAN PUBLISHING COMPANY
Gretna 2005

*The word "Pelican" and the depiction of a pelican are trademarks
of Pelican Publishing Company, Inc., and are registered in
the U.S. Patent and Trademark Office.*

Library of Congress Cataloging-in-Publication Data

Kissinger, Barbara Hallman.
  Christmas past / by Barbara Hallman Kissinger.
      p. cm.
  ISBN-13: 978-1-58980-356-5 (hardcover : alk. paper)
  1. Christmas in art. 2. Christmas—History. 3. Illustration of books. 4. Magazine illustration. I.
Title.
  NC968.5.C45K57
760'.04493942663—dc22

                                                                        2005011585

Text on page 17 excerpted from JOY TO THE WORLD: A VICTORIAN CHRISTMAS
    Copyright © 1990 by Cynthia Hart and John Grossman Inc., The Gifted Line
    Used by permission of Workman Publishing Co., Inc., New York
    All Rights Reserved

Text on page 23 from THE CHRISTMAS TREE BOOK by Phillip V. Snyder.
    Copyright © 1976 by Phillip Snyder.
    Used by permission of Viking Penguin, a division of Penguin Group (USA) Inc.

Printed in Singapore

Published by Pelican Publishing Company, Inc.
1000 Burmaster Street, Gretna, Louisiana 70053

To my grandchildren and great grandchildren: Troy, Sunshine, Jessica, Ben, Kyle, Ariel, Wesley, Nathan, Kyree, Kelli, Jackson, Koen, and Gracie

Many thanks to LaVon Worley and his class at SCC

Vintage postcard marked PFB
Printed in Germany, postally used 1909

Fröhliche Weihnachten!

E·KUTZER·

German Christmas
season figures
Vintage postcard
Postally used 1920

CONTENTS

Vintage postcard
Postally used 1908

The Norseman's Christmas *from* The Pictorial World,
December 25, 1875

INTRODUCTION

Christmas, the most celebrated holiday in the Christian world, is steeped in customs, traditions, and symbols. You might wonder where the world's Christmas customs originated. Many of the traditions that are such a treasured part of this season are rooted in pagan celebrations. In the first centuries, the Christian church, in order to find acceptance by the general population, adopted some of these ancient customs so that the beliefs and practices of Christianity would be more acceptable to the followers of the old religions.

Of the many pagan customs that eventually became the foundation of the Christmas season, many were adapted by the Christians from Norse mythology. The celebration of the Yule month, or Thor's month, began on the longest night of the year, referred to by the name of Mother Night. (Some historians think that Mother Christmas, the female counterpart of Father Christmas, descended from the name of this night.) The festival was called Yule, meaning wheel, because the sun was supposed to resemble a wheel rapidly revolving across the sky. The month of Yule was a time of feasting and rejoicing, according to the book *Myths of Northern Lands*, for it heralded the return of the sun. When Christians began to convert the northern peoples of Europe, missionaries, perceiving the extreme popularity of this time of feasting and celebration, thought it best to encourage the feast, but they claimed the drinking as a celebration to the health of the Lord and his twelve apostles. A celebration similar to Thor's feast has continued throughout the centuries.

Aspects of this Norse festival became so integrated with the Christian celebration that today, the word Yule is equated with the Christmas season. The Norse god Thor and his father Odin, or

Bringing in the Boar's Head
from The Illustrated London News,
December 23, 1871

The Gathering of the Mistletoe *from* The Illustrated London News, *July 13, 1895*

Woden (his Anglo-Saxon name), who were celebrated during this month, are the source of many Christmas traditions. Christmas revelers in medieval England, following a tradition rooted in the celebration of Thor's feast at Yule time, brought boar's heads to large Christmas feasts in the castles. In other parts of Europe, Christmas lore arose around personal characteristics of the Norse gods. Thor was known to travel through the skies in a cart or wagon pulled by two goats, and the European gift givers had been known, in centuries past, to sometimes travel on or with a goat, a custom probably originating with Thor. Odin traveled on his eight-legged horse Sleipner through the skies of the pagan world. This Norse influence can be seen in the Netherlands, where St. Nicholas, the Bishop of Myra, traveled on a white horse, delivering gifts to good children on the eve of his feast day, December 6.

Norse custom also provided the origins of decorating with evergreens, a symbol of eternal life. This practice was common among other cultures as well. The Druids, Celtic priests, also used evergreens, ivy, and mistletoe in their winter solstice celebrations during the month we call December. The Druids harvested mistletoe by cutting it down with a golden sickle in a grand ceremony.

Another culture that contributed to the modern celebration of Christmas was that of the Romans. Saturnalia, the most celebrated festival of the Roman Empire, began December 17 and lasted for a week. Not only did celebrants use greenery in the festival's decoration, but at this time of year they participated in some of the earliest gift giving in history.

Gift giving also occurred in other areas of the continent. Women of Norse and Germanic mythology were gift givers in some legends of Europe. Prechta, a legendary gift giver in the areas around Germany, was even known to accompany the Christ child on Christmas Eve to help deliver presents. However, this aspect of her legend did not develop until after the Reformation of the sixteenth century.

With the birth of Christ and the development of the Christian religion, the dominance of the old religions began to wane. According to the *Encyclopedia Britannica,* a Christmas celebration was held as early as 336 A.D. in the Eastern Roman Empire.

After the decline of the popularity of Roman and Greek gods, St. Nicholas, the Bishop of Myra, was adopted during the fourth century by the Roman Catholics. He replaced Neptune and Poseidon as an angel of the sea. Nicholas rose to sainthood by performing at least twenty-one miracles of the sea and mankind. Stories of St. Nicholas's miracles were spread by the sailors of the Mediterranean as they worked on boats that traveled the rivers of Europe.

In past centuries St. Nicholas was the third most revered Christian figure after Jesus and the Virgin Mary. St. Nicholas was even named the patron

Prechta, or Holda, and the Christ child
Vintage postcard, signed "Mailick"
Printed in Germany, postally used 1900

saint of Russia. He was the patron saint of many groups, including sailors, pawnbrokers, bakers, merchants, and children. Throughout the centuries, St. Nicholas also became the original Santa Claus to children of Europe. Children across Europe put their shoes out for St. Nicholas to fill with goodies of fruit, nuts, and sweets on the eve of his feast day.

It was Christianity that brought most of the gift givers to Europe. Some say the first Englishman who converted to Christianity was King Bran, around 60 A.D. King Bran brought his beliefs back to England after being taken hostage by the Romans, who then sent him to Rome where he learned of the new religion. But Christianity didn't really spread throughout England until the sixth century, with the help of the king of Kent. St. Patrick brought the religion to Ireland in the fifth century.

France also embraced Christianity in the fifth century, during the reign of Clovis, the King of the Franks. St. Boniface brought it to Germany in the eighth century. The peoples of what are now Bulgaria, the former Czechoslovakia, and the former Yugoslavia were converted to Christianity by two brothers, Cyril and Methodius of Greece. Vladimir I of Russia brought Christianity and the legend of St. Nicholas to his country in the latter part of the tenth century.

During the early Middle Ages, Epiphany (January 6), or Twelfth Night, as it was known in some places in Europe, was more celebrated than Christmas itself. Great feasts were held with wild celebrations. Gifts were given as the three Magi did when they found the baby Jesus.

Martin Luther, during the Reformation of the sixteenth century, broke away from Catholic dogma and established the Protestant side of the Christian religion. The Christ child became the gift giver in many Protestant parts of Europe; however, he was sometimes accompanied by traditional regional helpers.

You will learn more about the European gift givers later in this book. This book also has a section on the rise of Santa Claus in America and includes

some history of the symbols of Christmas. For fur-
ther reading on the historical development of
Christmas and its traditions, refer to the Further
Reading Guide at the end of this book.

This preamble hopes to lead you into discover-
ing the history as well as the beautiful and historical images throughout *Christmas Past*. The
imagery is from the author's collection of "Golden
Age" (1898-1918) Christmas postcards and old
Christmas cards, trade cards, and book and newspaper illustrations of the late nineteenth and early
twentieth centuries.

Vintage postcard marked PFB Serie 11060
Printed in Germany, postally used 1910

St. Nicholas, Bishop of Myra, 1660 Engraving
Original painting by Veronese

CHRISTMAS PAST

A MERRY CHRISTMAS

Vintage postcard
ca. 1910

HERALDING ANGELS

It was the heralding angels that came to tell the shepherds about the "Newborn King."

And there were in the same country shepherds abiding in the field, keeping watch over their flocks by night. And, lo, the angel of the Lord came upon them, and the Glory of the Lord shone round about them: and they were sore afraid. And the angel said unto them, Fear not: for, behold I bring you good tidings of great joy, which shall be to all people. For unto you is born this day in the City of David a Saviour, which is Christ the Lord. And this shall be a sign unto you; Ye shall find the babe wrapped in swaddling clothes, lying in a manger.

—Luke 2:8-12

Christmas postcards depicted this biblical scene. The representations were not plentiful, but some are still available for the Christmas collector.

Vintage postcard marked Serie 702
Printed in Germany, postally used 1910

Vintage postcard marked K. N.
Postally used 1935

MESSENGERS FROM HEAVEN

Swedish greeting
Vintage postcard
Marked A. V. Kbh
ca. 1905

Messengers from heaven are at the heart of the Christmas season. Angels have been part of the Christmas tradition since the birth of Christ, but the presentation of angels in art has developed throughout several centuries.

"White apparel" was the dress of the angels, according to the New Testament. Known to appear in human form when they came to earth, angels were first thought of as young men, especially in the Bible, but they eventually became more feminine through artistic renderings.

It was in the fifth century when heavenly angels first seemed to don wings. The lowest level of angels, those who communicated with people on earth, had to have some form of wings for flying as messengers between heaven and earth. In artistic portrayals, angels were also sometimes given halos to show their goodness and innocence.

In the mid-eighteenth century angels in paintings became even more beautiful and decorative. They began to appear in architecture of the time,

Vintage postcard
Marked EAS
Printed in Germany
ca. 1910

Vintage postcard marked PFB Serie 5401, ca. 1910

often as cherubs. During the Victorian period (mid- and late nineteenth century) children were often protected by pictures of guardian angels on their bedroom walls.

The popular use of angels continued through the end of the Victorian period, when angelic images became collectible. Postcards of angels were plentiful and many people collected them for their scrapbooks during the height of the German lithographic postcard period, or the "Golden Age of Postcards," 1898-1918. In the lore of some countries in Europe, such as Germany, Austria, and Italy, the Christ child brought gifts for children on Christmas Eve. The postcards of this period depicted that tradition, and the Christ child was often represented by a young female angel. The Christmas angels in these depictions were frequently shown with the Christmas tree, another Christmas symbol.

The connection between angels and Christmas trees that was apparent during this era began much earlier. The Nuremberg Angel, which topped many a Christmas tree in Victorian times, was created by a German doll maker who had lost his daughter during the Thirty Years' War (1618-1648) in central Europe. He created his angel out of tinsel. Other doll makers adapted his creation and began to make angels with spun glass wings, wax heads, and crinkled skirts. Some of the later ones had china heads, gold foil-pleated skirts, and shimmering foil wings.

Today angels are closely associated with the spirit of the Christmas season. In the book *Joy to the World: A Victorian Christmas*, the author states:

> In the December 1893 Christmas issue of *Ladies' Home Journal*, in a column entitled "The True Spirit of Christmas" the editors reminded the readers "Children are God's own angels sent by him to brighten our world, and what we do for these messengers from the sky, especially at that time of year which belongs to them, will come back to us threefold, like unto bread cast upon the waters."

This is a wonderful thought that captures the spirit of the Christmas season.

*Vintage postcard marked PFB
Printed in Germany, ca. 1910*

*Italian greeting, vintage postcard
Postally used 1922*

*Vintage postcard
Postally used 1912*

THE CHRISTMAS CRIB

The first Nativity scene was created by St. Frances of Assisi in the year 1223 at Greccio in Italy. He wished to inspire the people of Greccio and the surrounding territory to more religious involvement in Christ's birth. He fashioned a stable; stocked it with an ox, a donkey, and fodder;

The Vigil of St. Francis, Christmas Eve 1223 *from* Frank Leslie's Illustrated Newspaper *Christmas Number 1886*

Vintage postcard
Marked B. W. Christmas
Printed in Germany, postally used 1913

and created a manger with a doll-like figure of baby Jesus. Religious figures and peasants from around the area arrived to hold candles and torches to light up the night. St. Francis recreated that night at Bethlehem with his vibrant storytelling. The people responded exuberantly to his enthusiasm for the birth of Christ; they felt like they, themselves, were in Bethlehem observing the night of all nights.

The popularity of the Nativity spread. In France the Nativity display was called the *Creche* (cradle). In Italy it was called the *Praesepe* (manger). In Spain it was called the *Nacimiento* (nativity scene) and in Germany the *Krippe* (crib).

During the Renaissance artists created elaborate Nativity dioramas with great landscapes and numerous figures, including merchants and peasants in everyday settings. Ornate costumes adorned dolls in some of the figural scenes. The intricate displays detracted from the manger settings, but paintings of the Nativity were even more beautifully and ornamentally depicted.

It became quite common in the seventeenth and eighteenth centuries for churches to have their own Creche during the Christmas season. Families were also creating their own scenes in their homes. The wealthy used more elaborate figural settings with dressed miniature figures,

Vintage postcard, printed in France, ca. 1935

German greeting, vintage postcard, ca. 1906

while the poor families created theirs with small clay statues.

In Germany, a Christmas tree was set on a table in the parlor and a Krippe was placed under the tree. In other European countries, such as Russia and Czechoslovakia, children carried around a recreation of the Nativity in a box. They would sing carols while they went from house to house. The villagers they visited would give the children treats of cookies, fruit, or nuts.

German Christmas scene
Origin unknown, ca. 1900

Czechoslovakian Nativity
Vintage postcard, ca. 1933

Vintage postcard, ca. 1908

THE CHRISTMAS STAR

When one thinks of a star, one recalls childhood memories of "Twinkle! Twinkle! Little Star, how I wonder what you are!" or "Star Light! Star Bright! First star I see tonight." But these rhymes do not refer to a particular star in the sky. Rather these favored rhymes of childhood pale in comparison to the lore associated with a much different star, the Christmas star, which heralded Christ's birth.

Vintage postcard marked Serie 1480a
Printed in Germany, ca. 1912

Vintage postcard marked L & E
Serie 2264, postally used 1915

The Christmas star, which sparkles brightly at the top of many Christmas trees, is a Christian symbol of the Star of Bethlehem that led the three Magi to the Christ child. The various shapes of the star represent the life and spirit of Christ.

◆ The four-pointed star was sometimes used by artists to show Christ's star, since it took the form of a cross.

◆ The five-pointed star is the Star of Bethlehem, the Christmas star, standing for peace, goodwill, love, joy, and faith divine.

◆ The six-pointed star stands for the six days of creation. The Star of David also has six points.

◆ The seven-pointed star is a representation of the gifts of the spirit of the Lord: wisdom, understanding, counsel, power, knowledge, fear of the Lord, and delight in the Lord.

◆ The eight-pointed star is for regeneration. Jesus was named and circumcised when he was eight days old.

◆ The nine-pointed star represents the nine fruits of the spirit: love, joy, peace, patience, kindness, goodness, faithfulness, gentleness, and self control.

◆ The twelve-pointed star symbolizes the Twelve Apostles and is also used at Epiphany, the twelfth day of Christmas.

Some countries have incorporated greater aspects of the Christmas celebration around the significance of the star. Poland is unusual for the prevalent place that the star held in its Christmas customs. In Poland, Christmas Eve traditionally was not celebrated until the first star was seen in the

Polish Starman, vintage postcard
ca. 1926

The Christmas Star: A pretty Polish Custom
from The Illustrated London News
December 22, 1906

night sky. In some sections of Poland, the Starman, a figure who, like St. Nicholas, questioned children on their knowledge of the Bible, brought gifts to children on Christmas Eve. He was sometimes accompanied by the Starboys. In other areas the Little Star, who represented the Star of Bethlehem, brought children their gifts on Christmas Eve.

Another custom in Poland was for the peasants to go around at Christmas time with a large lighted star, symbolizing the Star of Bethlehem. Three boys impersonated the three kings of the East, Caspar, Melchior, and Balthazar. The peasants would travel from house to house singing for small coins. The Starboys would also carry a miniature puppet show, in which the drama of the Nativity and other scriptural incidents were performed.

The star was adapted for the American Christmas in the mid-1800s. In *The Christmas Tree Book*, the author, Phillip Snyder, states, "The first Christmas tree in Williamsburg, Virginia, appeared in 1842." This tree was decorated "with popcorn, nuts, colored-paper decorations, and a gold star." This seems to be the first mention of a star at the top of a Christmas tree in America.

Vintage postcard, ca. 1905

Vintage postcard, ca. 1910

ST. LUCIA'S DAY

One festival of light that has been celebrated since the eleventh century in Sweden is St. Lucia's feast day, observed on December 13. The feast day begins the Christmas celebrations in this part of the world.

On St. Lucia's Day, one daughter of each family dresses in a white gown with a red sash at her waist. She also wears a crown of evergreens with a circle of lighted candles. In the morning she wakes the household by bringing buns or cookies and a beverage to her family members in bed.

St. Lucia was a medieval saint from Sicily. No one knows how the Swedes came to celebrate her feast day, but they do so with great acclaim. In years gone by, children of Sweden put out their shoes on the eve of December 13 in anticipation of St. Lucia's leaving them a little present. St. Lucia also has been known to bring gifts to children in Sicily and some northern regions of Italy on her feast day.

Swedish depiction of St. Lucia,
Vintage postcard, postally used 1916

Italian depiction of St. Lucia
Vintage postcard, postally used 1903

THE CHRISTMAS CANDLE

In the fourth century, fragments of candle holders were found in Egypt; candles first brought light to the darkness centuries before. In fact, the Celts used candles in their winter solstice celebrations in the centuries before the birth of Christ. There

Vintage postcard, ca. 1909

are also references to candles in the Bible; the Hebrews called them lamps. The wick candle was developed by the Romans, who used tallow from cattle and sheep suet. Romans gave gifts of candles during the Saturnalia celebration, which started on December 17 and lasted for nearly a week.

The Christian church also used candles in its rituals. Candlemas, celebrated on February 2, was the ceremony during which the Church blessed the candles that were to be used for the next year. According to the book *Christmas and Christmas Lore* by T. G. Crippen, the blessing often invoked during the Middle Ages was "In whatsoever place they shall be lighted or put, the devil may depart, and tremble, and fly away, with all his ministers, from that habitation, and not presume any more to disturb it." Candle ends of this period were preserved as charms of good luck for they had been lit from the pure flame of the Star of Bethlehem candle, which had been newly struck from flint.

There were many superstitions associated with candles. Candle drippings were used to tell fortunes. Hot wax would be dripped from a candle into a bowl of cold water. The form that the wax drop took determined its meaning. The form of a four-leaf clover could mean good luck, the form of a sun could mean a brighter tomorrow, and the form of a star could mean happiness. Bad luck might come in the form of crossed bones.

It was also believed that while burning candles on Christmas Eve it was safe to speak of evil spirits. In Norway if the Christmas candle would last to the morning after Christmas, then the oldest member of the family would put it out and smear the remaining wax on the plow, cattle, and poultry as a charm against bad luck.

People in Ireland and other parts of the world have burned Christmas candles in their windows as a symbol of hospitality. These candles were a way of welcoming Mary and Joseph in their journey. Candlelight symbolized Jesus, the Light of the World. People of Europe would light a large Christmas candle on Christmas Eve and burn it continuously through Christmas day. It was considered bad luck if the candle burned out before the end of that day. The candle was also burned on New Year's Eve and Twelfth Night.

Catholics sometimes formed their Christmas candle into a three-branched triangular shape to symbolize the Trinity. These candles were burned to the point where the three branches met, and then it was used to burn in the new year for good luck.

Vintage postcard
Marked ASB Serie 161
ca. 1910

Vintage postcard
Printed in Germany
ca. 1908

CHRISTMAS BELLS A-RINGING

Whether it was sleigh or church bells or the tinkle of the gift giver's bell, the Christmas season has been filled with the sound of bells throughout the centuries. Victor Hugo, French novelist and poet, said the ringing of the bells was "the opera of the steeples." It is believed church bells originated in the fifth century and were widespread by the tenth. Bells originated in pagan times when, together with other noisemakers, they were used to frighten away evil spirits.

Christmas Bells *by Edwin H. Blashfield, 1893*

Vintage postcard marked SB
Serie No. 7098, postally used 1912

Legend has it that bells rang all over the world when Christ was born. In some countries it was believed that Satan died the eve before Christ's birth. Bells tolled his death for an hour, until midnight, as they always did for a dying person. But at the strike of midnight, bells rang joyously, heralding Christ's birth.

During the Middle Ages, bells were highly regarded, and their dedication was almost like a baptism. Only high-ranking church officials were called on to perform the blessing or baptism of a bell. The bells were bathed in holy water, and

Christmas Bell-Ringers by F. Dadd, from The Illustrated London News, *Christmas Number 1883*

Private mailing card, postally used 1906

*Vintage postcard, printed in Germany
Postally used 1915*

some had inspirational inscriptions engraved into them. Prayers were offered so that the sound of the bells would gather the faithful, encourage their devotion, and drive away evil spirits.

In Europe it was once though that if one put his ear to the ground in places where valleys had been destroyed by earthquakes, one could hear bells ringing on Christmas Eve.

In England, bell ringers rang in the Christmas season on St. Thomas's Day, December 21. For whom did the bells toll? They tolled for the season of the Christ child.

In certain parts of Europe, St. Nicholas, the Bishop of Myra, arrived on the eve of December 6, his feast day, to bring gifts to the good children. In many places he rang a bell to announce his arrival.

The *Christkindl* (Christ Child) came to many homes on Christmas Eve in Germany and other countries such as Austria, Belgium, France, and Switzerland. He brought the Christmas tree, decorated it, and left gifts for the children. When he was finished, he rang a bell to let the children know he had visited. Didn't you, as a child, hear sleigh bells ringing outside your home after Santa had visited on Christmas Eve?

Vintage postcard, printed in Belgium, ca. 1940

Vintage postcard, printed in Germany, ca. 1930

BRINGING IN THE YULE LOG

In Europe, the bringing in of the Yule log was once the most important occasion on Christmas Eve. The custom was first mentioned in Germany in 1184. Some believe the Yule log had its roots in the Celtic celebration of the twelve days during the winter solstice, when the sun was thought to stand still. The Celts lit bonfires to help bring the return of the sun's longer days. However, it was during the Nordic Yule month, which honored Thor, that a huge log was burned throughout the longest night of the year. It was a bad omen to let the log burn out before the following dawn.

Different countries used different trees for the Yule log. The tree could be an oak, a birch, a fir tree, or a fruit tree. Some cultures uprooted the tree, others just cut a length of the trunk; it could

Christmas, The Yule Log, *English engraving, 1846*

be up to five feet long. They would position the log partially in the hearth, and as it burned it would be pushed forward into the fire. Larger ones were used in the hearths of castles. There was always great ceremony when bringing in the Yule log. Some logs were draped with flowers and sprigs of evergreen. Some ceremonies included pouring wine and other spirits over the log. Others were even topped with money, which was later distributed to the servants.

In places in France, as the Yule log was brought into the house, a carol was sung praying for good blessings for the homestead. The blessings called for the women and animals to bear offspring, the crops to flourish, and the wine keg to be full. Then the youngest child would sprinkle wine on the log in the name of the Father, the Son, and the Holy Ghost. The log was burned and the ashes were kept all year as a remedy for illnesses.

A French poet, Frederic Mistral, told of marching around the kitchen three times with the log before placing it on the hearth. His father asked

The Benediction of the Yule Log in Touraine [France], *from* The Queen, The Lady's Newspaper, *December 25, 1880*

for blessings of joy and for no deaths to occur in the family in the new year.

In other countries the Yule log was burned every evening from Christmas Eve through the twelve nights of Christmas. It was believed that the charred remains, or ashes, protected the house all year from lightning and the animals from diseases. If mixed with food for the animals, it would increase reproduction; if mixed with the soil, crops would abound. Some women kept fragments of the log until Epiphany (January 6, when the Magi brought the gifts to the Christ child) so their poultry would prosper. In some parts of Italy, the ashes of the huge Yule log were used to protect the people against hail.

In parts of Germany it was the custom to lay a large "block" of wood on the fire, and when it had burned slightly, the fire would be doused. The wood was then saved for when a storm was imminent, and it was lit again to protect against lightning. Ashes were also used to protect trees and crops from diseases and insects. A small remnant of the log was retained to start the Yule log the next Christmas Eve, which was customary in many countries.

In England and some other European countries, it was bad luck to give a fire start to neighbors and

Vintage Postcard, Raphael Tuck & Sons, Christmas Series 8005, chromographed in Saxony, ca. 1912

Vintage Christmas card Hand colored, ca. 1930

friends during the time between Christmas Eve and New Year's Day. This belief dated to the eighth century, when it was believed that the good luck of the household spirit could be carried away with the gift of fire from the fireplace.

In England the Yule log was sometimes referred to as the "Yule clog." Its good luck was not obtained if the person lighting it did not have clean hands. Robert Herrick, the English poet, wrote:

> Wash your hands or else the fire
> Will not tend to your desire;
> Unwashed hands, ye maidens know,
> Dead the fire, though ye blow.

According to other English superstitions of the Yule clog, it was bad luck for a squinting person to come into the house while the log was burning. Another bad omen was if a bare-footed person entered the home during this time.

The custom of the Yule log did spread to America, but is no longer practiced except in historical reenactments. The big hearths are no longer available as in years gone by, except maybe in the castles of Europe.

Preparing for Christmas Eve
from The Illustrated London News
December 19, 1888

The Yule Log in India, Bringing in the Ice *by Adrien Marie*
from The Graphic, *Christmas Number 1889*

THE GATHERING OF THE GREENS

Vintage postcard marked PFB
Printed in Germany, ca. 1910

The decking of halls and homes with evergreens dates to the Roman celebration of Saturnalia. During this celebration, from December 17 to December 23, Romans decorated their homes and temples with greenery in honor of the god Saturn.

In present-day practices, homes continue to be decorated with evergreens during the month of December. However, it was the custom of Christmases past not to bring the greens into the home until Christmas Eve.

In the development of the season's decorations, ivy once rivaled holly for a place in the decking of the halls, but the ivy was replaced in popularity. People related ivy to the Roman god of wine, Bacchus, and his wild merrymaking. In America ivy was replaced as a Christmas decoration in the last of the nineteenth century.

The greenery still used in modern Christmas decorations has a long connection with the holiday. According to T. G. Crippen in his book *Christmas and Christmas Lore*, the custom in western England was that "a maiden should adorn her bed with a sprig of berried holly on Christmas Eve; otherwise she might receive an unwelcome

Vintage postcard
Signed "Ellen H. Clapsaddle"
International Art Publ. Co.
Printed in Germany, ca. 1912

Decorating the Signboard *by Yeend King*
from The Graphic, *Christmas Number 1882*

Gathering Greens *by E. N. Downard from* The Illustrated London News *December 16, 1871*

visit from some mischievous goblin." Crippen goes on to say, "In Germany a sprig of church holly, that is, one which had actually been used in church decoration, was regarded as a charm against lightning."

Sprigs of evergreen boughs and holly later decorated many Victorian homes. Wreaths were also made in abundance to adorn doors, walls, and fireplaces. City and rural dwellers alike often ventured into the countryside to cut their Christmas greenery themselves; however they could also buy the greenery at a city street market.

Mistletoe, another traditional Christmas decoration, is harvested by various methods. Druids wore sprigs or wreaths of holly in their hair when they went into the forests to cut mistletoe from the sacred oak with a golden sickle. Other cultures considered it bad luck to cut the mistletoe with a knife, contrary to the ways of the Druids. The plant was to be struck from a tree with big sticks or tool handles, arrows, pistols, or rifles. In some places it was thought that since the mistletoe was a parasite, it should never touch the earth, and it was considered bad luck if it did so.

More lighthearted superstitions have also been attached to the mistletoe. Down through the centuries it was thought that a kiss under the mistletoe was good luck. During the Victorian period, men plucked a berry from the kissing bough for every stolen kiss. When the berries were gone, no more kisses were allowed.

There were different customs as to removing the

HARPER'S WEEKLY.

JOURNAL OF CIVILIZATION.

Vol. XIX.—No. 991.]   NEW YORK, SATURDAY, DECEMBER 25, 1875.   [WITH A SUPPLEMENT. PRICE TEN CENTS.

Entered according to Act of Congress, in the Year 1875, by Harper & Brothers, in the Office of the Librarian of Congress, at Washington.

SELLING CHRISTMAS GREENS—A SCENE IN RICHMOND, VIRGINIA.—Drawn by W. L. Sheppard.—[See Page 1050.]

Selling Christmas Greens in Richmond, Virginia *by W. L. Sheppard*
from Harper's Weekly, *December 25, 1875*

greens after Christmas. In England, the Twelfth Night was the time chosen for the greens to be cleared away. They would be left in a spot outside to decay; it was unlucky to burn them. Other cultures would leave the greenery in their homes until Candlemas, the fortieth day after Christmas.

Vintage postcard by John Winsch 1911
Printed in Germany, ca. 1912

Vintage postcard, printed in Saxony
ca. 1910

O' TANNENBAUM

The Christmas tree with its evergreen boughs trimmed in tinsel, baubles, ornaments, and twinkling lights is of unclear origins. It is a common belief that the custom began in Germany; however, there are several legends and claims about the source of the Christmas tree.

It is thought that the Christmas tree might have originated with the Yggdrasil tree of Norse mythology. This was the great ash tree, the Tree of Life or the tree that held together earth, heaven, and hell by its roots and branches. Others believe the Christmas tree was a descendent of the pine trees of the Roman Saturnalia, which were adorned with earthen images of the wine god Bacchus.

There is also the old German legend of the eighth-century figure, St. Boniface, who came upon a Druid sacrifice to one of the Celtic gods. St. Boniface chopped down the sacred oak tree they were worshipping, and it split into several sections, falling in different directions. In the midst of the splintered oak, a small, unharmed fir tree stood. St. Boniface told the Druids that it was Christ's Tree of Life and showed them the way to

Die cut
Printed in Germany
ca. 1900

Vintage postcard from Germany
Postally used 1910

Christianity. Was this the birth of the first *Tannenbaum* (German for Christmas tree)?

Some people believe the Christmas tree descends from the Paradise tree of the early mystery plays. Some of these plays depicted stories of Adam and Eve, and the Paradise tree, adorned with apples, symbolized the Garden of Eden.

A legend of Martin Luther's Christmas tree from the sixteenth century also offers an origin for the custom. Luther was said to have gone walking in the forest on Christmas Eve. As he walked among the many evergreen trees, he looked up at the sky. The stars were twinkling through the boughs of the trees, and the new blanket of snow sparkled in the quiet and peaceful night. He chopped down a little fir tree and took it home. He then decorated it with candles as a Christmas treat for his children.

The variety of stories surrounding the Christmas tree make it difficult to trace its source. Riga, the capital of Latvia, claims to have had the first Christmas tree in 1510. The Estonians claim they had them as

Vintage postcard, Raphael Tuck & Sons Christmas Series No. 136, printed in Saxony, Postally used 1908

Vintage postcard marked B. W. 322 Printed in Germany, ca. 1912

*Bringing Home the Christmas Tree by A. Hunt
from* The Illustrated London News
Christmas Number 1882

early as 1441. Since the Germans influenced the culture of the Baltic States as far back as the thirteenth century, the claims of these areas do not necessarily negate Germany as the source of the custom.

Some of the first Christmas trees were chopped off the top of larger trees and hung upside down from the ceilings of homes. They symbolized the Holy Trinity.

The first account of a German Christmas tree was in Strasbourg in 1605. It was said to have been decorated with paper roses (a symbol of the Virgin Mary), apples (originally used on the Paradise tree), wafers (of the Holy Eucharist), candles (symbolizing Jesus, the Light of the World), and sugar treats.

The Puritan period, which started in the seventeenth century, quieted the reports of Christmas trees until the nineteenth century. The Puritans quelled the celebrations of Christmas because they thought it had too many pagan roots.

In nineteenth century England, the monarchs easily embraced the tree as a holiday symbol. In December 1829, at a Christmas pageant for George IV, a table was decorated with three potted trees adorned with three tiers of different colored wax candles surrounded by presents for the children. Queen Victoria of England had her first Christmas tree as queen in 1841. Her husband, Prince Albert, had brought the custom from his homeland, Germany.

*Vintage postcard
Postally used 1923*

In Saxony (eastern Germany), during the early nineteenth century, a substitute for the Christmas tree was a wooden-formed pyramid decorated with evergreens, candles, and little paper decorations and kept from year to year, possibly a forerunner of the modern artificial tree. They were also used in England during the same period. (These trees are evident in the foreground of the illustration of the Berlin Christmas market.)

The first reference to a Christmas tree in America was in 1747 at a Moravian Church in Bethlehem, Pennsylvania, on Christmas day. However, it was a wooden pyramid tree like the ones in Saxony.

There is also a story of Hessian mercenaries celebrating Christmas Eve in 1776 around a Christmas tree, a custom they had brought from their homeland, Germany. There is no written account to validate this event.

The Pennsylvania Dutch referred to their Christmas trees as the "Kriss Kringle Tree" because, as in Germany, Kriss Kringle, or the Christ child, was attributed with bringing the tree to families on Christmas Eve. The Christ child, according to an old German legend, flew through the air on golden wings and caused the Christmas tree to magically bloom overnight with sweets, apples, and gifts. Kriss Kringle was a derivative of the word *Christkindl* (German for Christ child), which developed through the mingling of languages that occurred when the German settlers arrived in America and intermarried with the English.

It was in the mid-1820s before more references were made to Christmas trees in America. Even

The Christmas Market, Berlin *from* The Illustrated London News, *January 3, 1871*

the classic poem, *'Twas the Night Before Christmas*, written in 1823 by Clement C. Moore, does not make any reference to a Christmas tree, and it has survived as the most popular Christmas poem of all time. Nor were Christmas trees pictured in illustrated books of the poem until the latter half of the nineteenth century. In 1825 Philadelphia's *Saturday Evening Post* mentioned trees seen through the windows of some homes. At that time, the Christmas trees in Europe and America were small trees placed on tables. It was not until later in the nineteenth century that large trees placed on the floor were mentioned.

The delayed use of the Christmas tree by Americans is not evident today. Whatever the Christmas tree's origins, now it is second only to Santa Claus as a symbol of Christmas in America.

How very happy I should be
If you were only here with me
To help me light my candles
And play around my Christmas
—tree—

Vintage postcard, postally used 1924

Vrolijk Kerstfeest

Vintage postcard from the Netherlands, ca. 1912

WASSAILING

Wassailing means "drinking to ones health" and was largely an old English custom. One person would begin by saying the phrase "was haile," and the other person would rebound with "drinc-heil."

According to *A Book of Christmas* by T. K. Hervey, for the well-to-do the drink would consist of rich wine, highly spiced and sweetened, with roasted apples floating in it. The common people would drink ale. In earlier centuries wassail was sometimes referred to as "lambswool" because of its smoothness of taste. This drink was served throughout the twelve days of Christmas, but most commonly on New Year's Day.

In many poems and songs, the drink was said to be contained in a brown bowl. Carolers would take their wassail bowl, adorned with ribbons and sometimes a golden apple or decked with evergreens, and carry it to each of their neighbors. After singing their songs they would ask the neighbors to fill their bowl, or they would share their own drink. Sometimes they would carry a little box or pouch and ask for a few coins.

Wassailing was also practiced in the early American colonies, and the tradition lasted for several centuries. The custom faded away by the twentieth century, except in reenactments of earlier times.

Wassailing of the fruit trees, another old custom, is well described in *Chatterbox*, a children's book of 1889. Farmers would visit their orchards in the evening accompanied by their farm laborers and carrying a large pitcher or milk pail filled with cider and roasted apples. They would circle one of the best-bearing trees and drink to the following toast three times:

Christmas, The Waits, *Engraving, unknown date*

The Wassail Bowl *by John Gilbert*
from The Illustrated London News
December 22, 1860

Here's to thee old apple tree,
Whence thou may'st bud, and thou may'st blow,
And whence thou may'st bear apples enow.
Hats full! Caps full!
Bushel-basket sacks full!
And my pockets full too! Huzza!

Apparently the good spirit of the wassail toast positively influenced the treees because after the recitation of the toast, the remains of the wassailing liquor were thrown against them with the thought that it would bring about a fruitful year.

Wassailing the Apple Tree *from* Chatterbox, *1889*

CAROLING, CAROLING, CAROLING

The word "carol" originally meant a dance with singing, exemplified by the children's song "Ring Around the Rosey" to which children would move in a circular pattern.

Vintage postcard, ca. 1908

Carol Singing in Yorkshire, England
by John Gilbert, from The Illustrated London News, *December 21, 1864*

*German die cut
ca. early twentieth century*

The Christmas Waits Refreshing at a Night Stall *by George G. Kilburne from* Pears Christmas Annual, *1896*

In 1201 King John of England began paying his clerks a small amount of money to chant to him about Christ on Christmas day. Some historians think these chants were the beginning of caroling. By the sixteenth century caroling had been established as a festive custom in England. It is likely, though, that modern audiences wouldn't recognize any of the carols from that period.

In England waits, nighttime musicians and singers, wandered the streets until late into the night playing and singing Christmas carols.

During the early sixteenth century they not only performed Christmas carols but also watched over the darkened streets in a similar manner as the night watchmen. The waits seemed to have originated with Edward III, who reigned in England from 1327 to 1377, for he first hired a single "wayte," or minstrel, to entertain him at Christmas time.

There was also an old custom in England and some parts of Germany of singing carols from church towers. This tradition continued until the middle of

Singing Christmas Carols in Russia
from The Graphic, *December 29, 1883*

the nineteenth century. In France, caroling at Christmas time was popular around the fourteenth century. The custom in Russia and Poland, in the last of the nineteenth century, was for the peasantry to visit the local landowners from Christmas Eve through Twelfth Night. They would sing a carol, called "Kolenda," while showing a box containing a representation of the Nativity.

Vintage postcard marked Series No. 1122
Printed in Germany, postally used 1910

Vintage postcard, International Art Publishing Co.
Marked New York-Phila. 1021, ca. 1912

VESSELS OF THE GIFT GIVER'S GIFTS

In America the most well-known vessels of Santa's gifts have been the Christmas stockings that were hung on the fireplace in hopes of a visit by St. Nicholas.

No one seems to know how the custom began. Some believe it came from a legend of St. Nicholas, the bishop of Myra, pertaining to his impoverished friend. The friend could not afford a dowry for his three daughters. As a result they would be unable to marry and would have to enter into prostitution. St. Nicholas refused to allow this to happen, so one night, as all were sleeping,

Vintage postcard
ca. 1908

Vintage postcard
Postally used 1909

he threw three bags of coins into his friend's window. They landed in the daughters' stockings, which were hanging on the hearth to dry. Thus, the daughters were able to marry in dignity.

It was in a little booklet from *The Children's Friend* Number III called "A New-Year's Present to the Little Ones from Five to Twelve" that the first lithograph of Christmas stockings was seen in America. This was in 1821. The story line underneath the picture said, "Through many houses he has been, and various beds and stockings seen. Some, white as snow, and neatly mended, others, that seemed for pigs intended." In this lithograph, the stockings were placed on the bed posts, as in England, rather than upon the fireplace hearth.

Children were enticed by the promise of presents from a seasonal gift giver. In Pennsylvania, in the early nineteenth century, the children of the German settlers would leave out a large plate or basket for the Christkindl, the Christ child, to fill during his visit on Christmas Eve. There was also the mention of "setting out" their hats as a receptacle for presents. However, the traditions of

Vintage postcard, Raphael Tuck & Sons
Ever Welcome Series, printed in Germany
Postally used 1911

Vintage postcard marked B. W. 366
Printed in Germany, ca. 1912

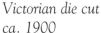

Victorian die cut
ca. 1900

Hanging Up the Stocking *from* The Night
Before Christmas, *ca. 1896*

Santa's gift bringing evolved to punish those who behaved poorly. If American children misbehaved, they would receive a piece of coal or a potato in their stockings.

European countries had several gift givers who arrived at different times during the holiday season. In accord with local customs, children used various receptacles for these gifts:

✦ In Belgium, on the eve of December 6, children would leave a little basket in anticipation that it would be filled with goodies and presents by St. Nicholas, the bishop.

✦ Croatians would leave their polished boots or shoes for St. Nicholas, hoping they would not get a golden rod that he sometimes left for the mischief makers.

✦ In the Slovonian and Dalmatian sections of

Christmas Eve—Hanging up the Stocking, *unknown origin, ca. 1879*

Croatia, St. Lucia would leave her presents on the eve of December 13 in a sock near the foot of the bed.

✦ Danish children of the sixteenth century would leave a bowl on a chair or table for the Christ child to leave the presents on Christmas Eve.

✦ In England, Ireland, and Wales, Father Christmas left small gifts in stockings at the foot of the children's beds.

✦ In France it was the children's shoes that were left out for St. Nicholas on the eve of December 6 or for Pere Noel on Christmas Eve.

✦ Some of the children of Estonia left their socks or shoes on the window sill so that elves could leave a little present each night of December until Christmas.

✦ In Hungary children would put their polished boots on the window sill for St. Nicholas to fill on the night of December 5.

✦ On St. Nicholas Eve in Luxembourg, the children would leave their slippers outside the bedroom door or leave a plate on the dining table.

✦ In the Netherlands, St. Nicholas Eve was the only time that children left their wooden shoes out to receive gifts. Christmas was not a time for gifts.

✦ In Poland, St. Nicholas would leave his presents in the children's polished boots or under their pillows.

✦ Romanian children would leave their boots or shoes on the window sill for St. Nicholas or in more recent times, at the main door of the home's entrance. He left an "adorning rod" for the disobedient.

✦ In Spain, Puerto Rico, and some parts of Portugal

and France, on the eve of January 6, Epiphany, the children would leave their shoes, filled with hay and carrots for the horses of the Magi, on the window sills or by the doorways. The wise men would reciprocate and fill the shoes with presents.

◆ Ukrainian gifts from St. Nicholas were sometimes left on plates, on windowsills, in shoes by the fireplace, or under the children's pillows.

However the spirit of the season is shared with children of each country, the tradition of gift giving during the Christmas season is one that children from around the world eagerly await.

Vintage postcard from Germany
Postally Used 1910

Vintage postcard
Postally used 1909

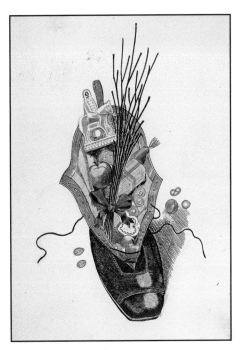

Vintage postcard
ca. 1908

Christmas Eve and Christmas Morning in France
from Harper's Young People, *unknown date*

Vintage postcard (England, Ireland, Wales)
Raphael Tuck & Sons, printed in Germany
Postally used 1909

Vintage postcard, German-American Novelty Art
Series, marked No. 1049, printed in Germany
ca. 1910

PRETTY PARCELS OF SURPRISE

Vintage postcard printed in Germany, ca. 1910

The history of those pretty parcels of surprise that have greeted excited children at Christmas time predates the Magi's gifts to the Christ child of gold, frankincense, and myrrh.

The Romans' January kalends festival was a time of gift giving in a Christmas-like setting. They decorated with greenery and lights. The citizens of Rome, including the Senate, were expected to give gifts of money to the emperor. Other gifts of goodwill and greenery between friends and neighbors were called *strenae*.

In the north, the goddesses of Norse mythology and Germanic legends would distribute gifts to their peasants or followers during the winter solstice. They rewarded the men for growing the flax and the women for spinning it into clothing and blankets. Frau Holda, a goddess of southern Germany, would come down into her villages in the evening hours between nine and ten with a wagon full of presents for the local peasants who

Vintage postcard Marked C-147 ca. 1912

Vintage postcard, printed in U.S.A. Postally used 1915

had shown her respect by spinning diligently.

Similar customs of gift exchange continued into the Christian era. In some European countries in the eleventh century, around the Christmas season, there was an interesting custom at harvest time. Children would ask the harvesters for a small coin for luck, and it was considered bad luck to refuse them.

Gift giving in France began about the twelfth century, when nuns would give poor children gifts of fruit and sweets around Christmas. In 1377, Charles V of France gave his court subjects gifts of gold, incense, and myrrh in gold cups. In the fourteenth century gifts also were given to kings and queens in Europe on New Year's Day; in return their subjects would receive money or gifts such as silver gilt basins and pitchers.

It was around that time when St. Nicholas started visiting children on the eve of his feast day. He would question the children on their catechism. If they had been good and knew their Bible lessons, he would reward them with fruit (mainly apples), nuts, and sweets. It was not until the twentieth century that he started leaving little presents other than fruits and sweets for the children. In some countries, St. Nicholas only left gifts for boys; St. Lucia was responsible for leaving the girls presents on her feast day, December 13.

In the sixteenth century in Germany, Christmas

Vintage postcard, printed in Germany, ca. 1912

Vintage postcard marked 450/3 No. 3812
Printed in Germany, postally used 1912

gifts for children were tied in bundles and always contained something nice, something useful, and something of discipline, like a rod or switch. It was also in Germany, according to Clement A. Miles in his book *Christmas In Ritual and Tradition*, that a common gift for German children at Christmas or New Year's Day was an apple with a coin in it; the coin may have conceivably been a Roman survival, while the apple was connected with those brought by St. Nicholas.

A present called a "Yule-Klapp" was given in Sweden and some parts of Germany. It was a present of jewelry or some other small gift. It would be

Vintage postcard, printed in Germany,
Postally used 1911

Vintage postcard from Czechoslovakia
Postally used 1912

Christmas Morning, *unknown origin*
Published 1904

packaged and wrapped in a small box that would be put in progressively larger containers, resulting in a large present. The giver of this gift would deliver it at night with a knock on the door of the intended recipient. He would then open the door, throw in the present, and run away as fast as possible so that his identity would not be detected until the recipient had opened the gift.

On Christmas Eve in Germany, the Christ child or his helper would sometimes leave his presents in the branches of the Christmas tree, which was placed on a table. A Nativity scene would be displayed on the table under the tree. The Pennsylvania Dutch's gift giver was also the Christ child, or the Christkindl, as the Germans called him. They called their presents "Christ Kindly," a

Father Christmas in England
Unknown origin, 1906

Vintage postcard, German-American Novelty Art Series, marked No. 1048 (6 Des.) printed in Germany, postally used 1912

In America, it was the last half of the nineteenth century that gift giving shifted from New Year's Day to Christmas, as we now celebrate it.

derivative of their name for the baby Jesus.

One holiday custom in England was for families to give Christmas hampers to friends. The hamper could be of wicker, the size of a picnic basket or larger. It would contain several types of foodstuffs, even the Christmas poultry, and possibly other presents and a bottle of spirits.

At children's parties or social gatherings in England in the nineteenth century there was a custom of having a lucky tub or a bran tub. This tub might be a wooden barrel decorated lavishly in ribbons, ruffled skirts, and bows. The tub would be filled with bran, paper, or wood shavings within which gifts were hidden. The children would line up and take a turn dipping into the tub to retrieve a gift.

The Lucky Tub *by Mary L. Gow*
from The Graphic, *Christmas Number 1894*

The Bran Tub, *Book annual from England, 1908*

CHRISTMAS TRADE CARDS

The American trade card experienced its greatest popularity in the late nineteenth century. These cards were used to advertise products and stores in Victorian America. The Christmas trade cards, made by the chromolithography process, were the most sought-after because they were placed in the scrapbooks of many Victorian families.

One could follow the development of Santa's image by means of the Santa trade cards. Other Christmas trade cards showed winter scenes, children at play, Christmas trees, and toys. The

Thea-Nectar Tea, The Great Atlantic & Pacific Tea Co., ca. 1900

Gooch's Prescription, The Cincinnati Drug & Chemical Co., ca. 1900

images would appear on the front of the card, and the advertisements were printed on the blank backside. Companies advertised an array of products, such as medicinal remedies, teas, coffee, or plum puddings, on their trade cards. Some images on the front also included space for the name and address of the store.

Some of the most popular trade cards were those produced by Woolson Spice Company of Toledo, Ohio. Their colorful images were often placed on the front of cards for the highly advertised Lion Coffee.

In this section, images of chromolithographic Christmas trade cards are pictured. Each card advertises various products on the back. One back image is shown as a sample. The cards were placed on store counters and left for customers to pick up. Others were found in the tins and boxes of various products, such as teas and coffees.

Lion Coffee, *Woolson Spice Company* ca. 1900

St. Claus' Greeting, *Beer and Schweitzer* ca. 1900

Lion Coffee, *Woolson Spice Company* ca. 1900

*Lion Coffee, Woolson Spice Company
ca. 1900*

*Lion Coffee, Woolson Spice Company
ca. 1900*

*Anchor Coffee, Boos &
Holbrook, ca. 1900*

Lion Coffee, Woolson Spice Company
ca. 1900

Back image for Lion Coffee, Woolson Spice
Company, ca. 1900

Cherry Pectoral, Dr. J. CA. Ayer & Co.
ca. 1900

CHRISTMAS GREETINGS

Before the Christmas holiday was popularized, New Year's Day was the celebrated mid-winter festival, and New Year greetings originated in Europe around 1466, hundreds of years earlier than the first Christmas cards. Though in celebration of a new year, one such greeting was an engraving of the Christ child.

The design of the first Christmas card has been attributed to John Calcott Horsley in 1843 in England. Designed at the request of his friend Henry Cole, there were approximately one thousand cards made.

By the late nineteenth century, there were several Christmas greeting card producers in England, Germany, and America.

Louis Prang, known as the father of the American Christmas card, came to America in 1850 from Breslau, Silesia, part of modern-day Poland. Prang began selling his Christmas cards in America around 1875. In the 1880s he hosted art

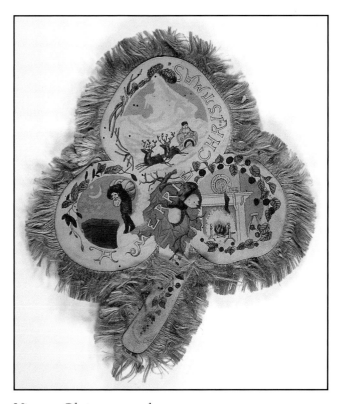

Vintage Christmas card
ca. 1870s

Vintage Christmas card, W. Hagelberg
ca. 1890

Vintage Christmas card, Prang & Co., printed in Boston, ca. 1880s

Vintage Christmas card, printed in England, ca. 1880s

competitions in order to find designs for his Christmas greetings. The resulting cards were works of fine art. He was producing around five million Christmas cards a year by 1881; however, the German "Golden Age Postcards" eventually replaced Prang's cards. The German postcards were less expensive and because they did not need envelopes, their postage was less costly.

Vintage Christmas card, W. Hagelberg, printed in Germany, ca. 1880s

Vintage Christmas card, Raphael Tuck & Sons
Printed in England, ca. 1880s

Vintage Christmas card, Raphael Tuck & Sons, printed in England, ca. 1880s

CHRISTMAS WISH:

MUCH LOVE AND HAPPINESS

TO YOU!

Vintage Christmas card, Prang & Co.
Printed in Boston, copyright 1881

Vintage Christmas card, Marcus Ward
& Co., printed in England, ca. 1880

THE GIFT GIVERS OF EUROPE

AUSTRIA

St. Nicholas, called St. Nikolo by the Austrians, visited children on his feast day, December 6, accompanied by Krampus. Krampus, who punished naughty children, was an ugly, hairy beast with horns and a long red tongue, much like the common image of the devil. St. Nicholas listened to the children's prayers and lessons. He would review their behavior, which had been recorded in a large book by guardian angels, who kept track of the good and bad deeds of the children throughout the year. If the children had been good and knew their lessons, St. Nicholas rewarded them with sweets, nuts, or fruit.

On Christmas Eve, Christkindl, the Christ child, came down from heaven with his band of angels. Christ, however, was portrayed by a girl with wings like an angel who brought a decorated tree and presents for the children. When the children heard the tinkling of a bell on Christmas Eve, they knew that the Christ child had been to their home. The parents would then take the children into the previously closed parlor. There the Christmas tree and presents waited.

St. Nikolo and Krampus
Vintage postcard, postally used 1918

Christkindl and his band of angels
German magazine illustration, 1896

71

Svaty Mikulas
Vintage postcard
Postally used ca. 1920

CZECHOSLOVAKIA

More than a century ago in Czechoslovakia, the celebration of the Advent season started on the fourth of December with the feast day of St. Barbara, a martyr from the time of the Roman persecutions of Christians. For many rural villages, the saint was the first gift giver of the season. In Czechoslovakian lore, St. Barbara dressed in a white cloak and wore a green wreath over her long, flowing hair. She carried switches for the disobedient children and a basket of fruit and nuts for the good children. To announce her arrival, she would tap on the window of a home. In some regions, St. Barbara was accompanied by people disguised as goats or devils.

On December 6, Svaty Mikulas (St. Nicholas) brought presents for the good children in Czechoslovakia. He was believed to climb down from heaven on a golden rope or cord and would wander through the villages and countryside. His companions, an angel and a whip-carrying devil called Cert, followed him everywhere. In anticipation of their arrival, the children would leave their shoes or boots on the windowsill or doorsteps for Svaty Mikulas and the angel to fill with goodies for the good children or coal for the roguish children. The devil's duty was to punish naughty children; he would scare them and threaten to take them away from their parents. So that they would be visited by Mikulas instead of Cert, children would have to promise to be good for the whole year.

In later years, Jezisek (baby Jesus) would bring gifts on Christmas Eve. After dinner that night, the family would close the room with the Christmas tree so that the baby Jesus could bring presents. Jezisek would ring a bell before he left to let the children know he had been there.

DENMARK

In Denmark, by the early part of the nineteenth century, there was a mythical creature of tiny stature like an elf, called a *nisse*. The nisse was hundreds of years old and had a white beard, gray shirt and trousers, a red cap and stockings, and wooden shoes. No one ever saw the creature, but sometimes his steps could be heard at night, when he walked around watching the farm or the house and especially the animals, as he was able to speak their language. The nisse must be given food and treated well; if not, he would let all manner of bad things happen to families. The cows would give no milk, someone could fall and break a leg, or worst of all, children could get ill if a family failed to properly treat the nisse.

Regarding the nisse, the Danes had a nice tradition for Christmas night. They placed a bowl of rice pudding in the barn loft for him. There was to be a good lump of butter and sugar mixed with cinnamon on top of the pudding, as well as a glass of sweet beer to accompany the meal. This treat was to pacify the nisse so that he would not cause trouble.

In the last half of the nineteenth century, Santa Claus began showing up in Denmark, a figure that spread from Germany. He was called Julemand (the Christmas man). Over the years he became connected with the nisse, who suddenly then were called the Julenisse (the Christmas nisse). However the nisse was not the one to bring gifts.

The Julemand was believed to live in Greenland, and children would write letters to him with their wishes for Christmas. He brought the gifts on Christmas Eve when the family was gathered around the Christmas tree. Unfortunately, Daddy was not present at this happy moment as he was suddenly called away. But the Julemand was kind enough to leave some gifts for Daddy to have when he returned.

Julemand
Vintage postcard
Postally used 1910

ENGLAND

Father Christmas, as the English gift giver has been known, seems to have originated in the old mummers' plays of the Middle Ages. The mummers' play was originally a folk drama, with roots more pagan than Christian. The play celebrated the return of spring after the long winter, a symbolic return to life after death. One of the better-known mummers' plays was about St. George and the Dragon. Father Christmas introduced the characters in the play and set the scenes. He was known then as Christmas, Old Christmas, Mr. Christmas, or Captain Christmas, and ordinarily only men performed the roles.

The appearance of Father Christmas as he is known today was largely created when Charles Dickens wrote *A Christmas Carol* in the 1840s, and John Leech created the illustrations of the holiday figure. From those illustrations Father Christmas became known as a tall, statuesque gentleman with a long green robe, a crown of holly, a long beard, and long hair. Though in the latter part of the nineteenth century the color of his robe changed to red, and Father Christmas gave up the crown of holly for a red hood, he was still recognizable as the legendary figure created by Leech.

Father Christmas
Vintage postcard, Ernest Nister,
London, postally used 1909

Father Christmas
Vintage postcard, Raphael Tuck
& Sons, postally used 1904

Father Christmas
Vintage Christmas card
ca. 1900

ESTONIA

In some regions of Estonia, around the 1900s, the Christ child brought presents on Christmas Eve. This custom was likely a result of German influence.

However, during the Communist regime, Christmas was frowned upon. "New Year Claus," as the Estonians called him, was the gift giver on New Year's Eve. But some of the people of Estonia still managed to celebrate Christmas quietly in their churches and homes.

In more recent times, Santa Claus arrived by sleigh from Lapland. Everyone, in each household, had to perform for their gifts by reciting a poem, doing a dance, or singing a song.

Vintage postcard, postally used 1928

Vintage postcard, printed in Estonia
Postally used 1906

FINLAND

A long time ago, before the rise of Christianity, people of Finland were visited during the winter solstice by a very brash goat. This goat was called Joulupukki (pronounced u-lu-puki), which in Finnish meant "Yule buck." He always demanded presents, and families would gladly give him gifts in order to ensure the family's good health and a bountiful harvest in the coming year.

Over the years the goat mellowed, and he arrived around Christmas to make sure the children were obedient and well behaved. If he was satisfied that the children were deserving, he would toss presents onto the floor of the home. Around the end of the nineteenth century, Joulupukki transformed from a goat into a kindly old man, sometimes called Old Man Christmas, and he wore a gray sheepskin coat. A goat sometimes accompanied Joulupukki to carry the gifts.

In the first half of the twentieth century, Joulupukki was known to live in Korvatunturi Fell or Ear Mountain. It was named for the three peaks that looked like rabbit ears. Korvatunturi was in the Lapland area of Finland, north of the Arctic Circle. Father Christmas or Joulupukki began wearing a red coat during this period. He lived with his wife Mother Christmas and his helpers, the elves. The elves were sometimes dressed in red and blue, the colors of Lapland. Their hats and tights were always in red, and the color of their jackets varied, but gray or blue were the more traditional colors.

The elves were called the *tontut*. They helped Joulupukki hand out the presents at each house where the children were found to be of good behavior. The tontut spied on the children all through the year and knew who was good or bad before they arrived on Christmas Eve. The obedient children received nice presents; naughty children received a bundle of twigs.

Vintage postcard, ca. 1920

Vintage postcard, postally used 1908

FRANCE

An old half-fairy, half-witch character called Tante Arie originated in Franche-Comte, a former province of France. Tante Arie lived in a cave and came down from the mountains on Christmas Eve or New Year's Eve with her donkey and spread joy for the good children by leaving candy, nuts, and fruit. She also carried switches for the mischievous children. She came in many disguises, and she had the feet of a goose. Arie's arrival was heard by everyone, for the bell around the donkey's neck would ring loudly. The children would leave out hay and salt, or carrots and turnips, much to the delight of Tante Arie's donkey.

In the northern part of France, as in other European countries, young children celebrated St. Nicholas Day on December 6. They left their shoes out on St. Nicholas Eve for the saint to fill with small toys and sweets. Beginning around the eighteenth century, Pére Fouettard (Father Spanker or Father Whipper) accompanied St. Nicholas to take care of the troublesome children.

In Alsace, the gift giver was Christkindl, also called Frau Berchta as in some parts of Germany, for Alsace was once a part of that country. Christkindl, the Christ child, was represented by a young girl, a parallel to St. Lucia of Sweden, with a crown of four lighted candles. She represented light and was accompanied by Hans Trapp, a horrible character who disciplined and scared disobedient children. He would supposedly take them into the forest, and they would never be seen

again. Hans Trapp was sometimes described as dressing in a bearskin or animal skin with a blackened face and long beard and carrying rods or chains with which to beat the children. Sometimes a donkey called Peckersel followed along with, or carried, Christkindl. Pére Fouettard sometimes accompanied Christkindl near the border with Germany.

Near the border with Spain, on the eve of January 6 children kept watch for the three Magi, the gift givers of that region. The children would leave hay out for the wise men's camels.

Another gift bringer in France was Le Petit Jesus (baby Jesus). It was thought that the baby Jesus was the one for children to pray to and ask for presents on Christmas Eve or January 6. In the middle of the twentieth century, children believed the heavens opened and baby Jesus came down to bring their presents.

Over the last century, the main gift giver of France has been Pére Noel (Father Christmas). In some areas he came on December 6, and again on Christmas Eve. Sometimes accompanied by Pére Fouettard, Pére Noel traveled with a donkey at times; sometimes he just carried his bag of toys. In other areas, he transported his gifts on his back in a grape-gathering basket, which was a symbol of the vineyards of France. Pére Noel has been described in the last half century as wearing a long red robe with a hood, all trimmed in white fur.

Baby Jesus, vintage postcard ca. 1910

Frau Brechta in Alsace
from The Queen, the Lady's Newspaper,
December 25, 1880

Pére Noel
Vintage postcard
ca. 1910

Three Magi
Vintage postcard
ca. 1920

GERMANY

On St. Nicholas Eve, December 5, Sankt Nikolaus would come to listen to the children's prayers, Bible verses, and hymns. Sometimes he would give them nuts, fruit, or sweets for the correct answers. Other times he would come back after the children had gone to sleep and leave his gifts.

The sound of a bell would announce St. Nicholas's arrival. His mode of transportation varied: he was known to travel by donkey, white horse, goat, or foot. At times, he would carry a book of the children's good and bad deeds.

Receptacles for the gifts of the old saint varied. Some children would leave a bowl or plate under the bed or hang a stocking by the fireplace. Others would leave their shoes or boots under the bed or outside the bedroom door, on their windowsill or by the fireplace, or even on the front doorstep for St. Nicholas to fill. Parents would tell their children to shine their shoes before putting them out so that they would impress the generous saint.

In days of old, an assistant accompanied St. Nicholas who would take care of the naughty children while the old saint took care of the good children. The assistant carried rods or switches to disperse punishment. He also carried a bag in which to stuff the naughty children. He went by different names, depending on which German region he frequented.

With Martin Luther and the Reformation of the sixteenth century, the characteristics of St. Nicholas were transformed. Luther took away the ecclesiastical clothing of St. Nicholas, and in northern Germany the figure became Pelznichol, meaning fur-clad St. Nicholas. He

St. Nicholas's visit, German magazine illustration, ca. 1900

accompanied the Christ child, who became the gift giver for Christmas. German children of Protestant families then received their presents on Christmas Eve.

Among Catholics in Germany, Knecht Rupecht, or Farmhand Ruprecht, was a favorite companion during St. Nicholas's December 5 visits. The Protestants also adopted Ruprecht as a companion to the Christ child. First mentioned as Christ's servant (his name means "the servant") in a seventeenth century Nuremberg Christmas procession, Knecht Ruprecht's legend sometimes merged with that of Der Weihnachtsmann (the Christmas Man), another character who accompanied the Christ child on Christmas Eve.

Eventually the Weihnachtsmann brought the presents by himself. In time he took on an appearance similar to that of Father Christmas of England or Santa Claus of the United States. The Christ child, or Christkindl, as the German children called him, still brings gifts in the southern part of Germany, and St. Nicholas Eve, December 5, remains a part of Germany's celebration of the holiday season.

*Pelznichol and the Christ child
Vintage postcard, ca. 1920*

*Knecht Ruprecht, German magazine
illustration, 1882*

*Christkindl and Knecht Ruprecht, German
magazine illustration, 1899*

The Christmas Man, vintage postcard
Postally used 1939

Der Weihnachtsmann, vintage postcard
Postally used ca. 1915

The Christmas Man, vintage postcard
Postally used 1923

HUNGARY

Hungary has practiced holiday traditions similar to those of other European countries. The Hungarians also celebrate the feast day of St. Nicholas, who is called Szent Mikulas in that region. Sometime around the thirteenth and fourteenth centuries, St. Nicholas began arriving at the doors of children's homes on the eve of his feast day. He checked on the children to see if they were learning their Bible verses and showing respect to their elders. Good and obedient children were rewarded with fruit and sweets. Naughty children were admonished by a devil-like character Hungarians called Krampusz, who accompanied St. Nicholas.

On Christmas Eve day the children were kept occupied by one parent while the other parent decorated the tree behind the closed doors of the parlor. Then presents were placed under the tree. In the evening the children waited for the ring of a bell, which revealed when the baby Jesus and/or the little angels had visited their home. The parents would open the doors to the parlor and the children would run gleefully in to find their presents under the tree.

During the last century, a character more like Santa Claus of the United States has begun to deliver presents for Christmas.

Krampusz and St. Nicholas
Vintage postcard, ca. 1910

Vintage postcard, printed in Austria
Postally used 1907

Baby Jesus, vintage postcard, ca. 1910

Szent Mikulas, vintage postcard
Postally used ca. 1910

ICELAND

In pre-Christian times, gifts were given by chieftains to their friends and guests at the Yule celebration. A gift of a candle for each member of a family was also among the first gifts of Yule since the light of several candles was brighter than the light of an oil lamp. After Christianity's arrival, it became customary for employers to give their employees a Christmas present of an article of clothing. This exchange was the only form of gift giving until the late nineteenth century, when a deck of cards became a common gift.

Gryla and Leppaludi, two trolls, appeared in thirteenth century Icelandic folklore. Gryla was very cruel in these tales for she was said to have caught and eaten naughty children. Even in more recent times, parents have threatened their children with punishment from Gryla.

By the seventeenth century Gryla had given birth to thirteen sons. They were called "Jolasveinar," or Yulemen. In the past they were known to wear woolen clothes of black, white, gray, or brown and lambskin. But as time passed, it became a popular tradition in the villages that the Yulemen wore more colorful red clothing. In more recent times, however, the people of Iceland describe them in the more subdued clothing of earlier centuries.

The thirteen Yulemen would venture down from the mountains, starting on December 12. One troll or Yuleman would enter each household each day until Christmas; therefore, every home would have a total of thirteen trolls or elves causing trouble by Christmas Eve. They were pranksters and very devilish in the early folklore, but over the centuries they became less mischievous.

The Yuleman eventually became responsible for leaving presents for children. Each night, beginning on the twelfth of December, children would put their shoes on the windowsill so that the Yuleman could leave a present for them. Some children would also leave a little present for the gift giver. Naughty children might receive a potato or nothing at all.

Families exchanged presents on Christmas Eve. On Christmas day the Yulemen started leaving the house, one each day, until all of them had returned to the mountains to await the next Christmas.

Vintage postcard
ca. 1915

ITALY

In Italy, gift givers have varied according to regions and local traditions. Largely celebrated along the Adriatic Coast, the first gift giver of the holiday season was St. Nicholas, who left gifts on his December 6 feast day. It was usually along the Adriatic Coast where St. Nicholas was celebrated. Little angels sometimes accompanied him. The saint listened to the prayers and lessons of the children and rewarded them with small presents, or sweets and fruit.

In Sicily, on the thirteenth of December, Saint Lucia's Day was observed. Saint Lucia brought gifts to the children of the island, while at times traveling on a donkey.

Years ago in Italy, depending on local tradition, adults exchanged gifts on January 1, as in the era of the Roman Empire, when citizens gave each other branches of greenery for good luck.

At the end of the nineteenth century, in northern regions near the border of Germany and Austria, the Christ child, accompanied by a helper, brought gifts on Christmas Eve. In these

Vintage postcard, postally used 1914

regions the Christ child was represented by a young female angel.

This custom spread to other regions in Italy beginning in the first half of the twentieth century. Here, too, baby Jesus was represented by a child or an angel as he brought gifts into homes on Christmas.

Around the middle of the twentieth century, Babbo Natale (old man Christmas or Father Christmas), brought gifts to some of the Italian children on Christmas Eve. This custom has increased in popularity over time.

The most well-known gift giver of Italy has been Befana, who came to children's homes on the eve of January 6. Her legend contends that the Magi stopped by her house while looking for the road that would lead them to baby Jesus. Befana told them to be on their way; she was cleaning her house and did not have the time to bother with them. After they left, guilt overcame her. Ever since that time, on the eve of January 6, she has sought to find the baby Jesus so she could help the three men in their search. In every house that she has visited during her quest, she has left presents for the children.

St. Nicolaus
Vintage postcard
Printed in Italy, ca.1920

Baby Jesus
Vintage postcard
ca. 1912

In past centuries, Befana was described as an old witch in black clothing who rode a broomstick. In more recent times, she has become a little more colorful in her costume. In some areas, the children have left their windows open for Befana to fly through and leave her gifts. In others, she flies down the chimney. She is known to leave lumps of coal or ashes for rebellious children.

Babbo Natale
Vintage postcard
ca. 1930

Befana
Vintage postcard
Postally used 1918

NETHERLANDS

In the Netherlands, St. Nicholas Eve, December 5, has been the most celebrated time in the Christmas season. The people of the Netherlands have held St. Nicholas in very high esteem, regardless of personal religious preference.

St. Nicholas, or Sinterklaas, as the Dutch call him, arrives in mid-November on his steamboat from Spain to a different port each year. His helpers simultaneously arrive all over the Netherlands. Sinterklaas carries a big red book listing all the good and bad children, and he is accompanied by his white horse and his assistants, the Zwarte Pieten. Sinterklaas's horse does not seem to have any particular name, but some people think he might have descended from Odin's mythical horse Sleipner.

The Zwarte Pieten are traditionally black faced and are believed to have descended from the Moors of Africa during the Netherlands' occupation by Spain in the sixteenth century. Their costumes are of the sixteenth century style consisting of short, puffed breeches, known as trunk hose, over tights. They also wear hats with a feather plume and bodices with long, puffy sleeves and a ruff at the neck.

In the latter part of the nineteenth century, Zwarte Piet (Black Peter) took care of the bad children. At this time he and Sinterklaas did not yet have helpers. In more recent times, Sinterklaas has many helpers to impersonate himself and Zwarte Piet. The children understand that they are needed since Sinterklaas can not be everywhere at once. The Zwarte Pieten are especially loved by the children of the Netherlands, even more so than Sinterklaas himself. They are the ones in this celebration that hand out the candies and trinkets at the parades in Sinterklaas's honor. The Zwarte Pieten are very sprightly, jumping around and entertaining the children.

During the night of December 5, legend has it that Sinterklaas and his white horse, along with

Sinterklaas and Zwarte Piet
Vintage postcard, ca. 1912

Zwarte Piet, travel over the rooftops of every Dutch family with children. Zwarte Piet descends each chimney, leaving presents from the old saint for the children. Zwarte Piet then ascends the chimney, much like Santa Claus does in America. In some homes, Sinterklaas has also been known to knock at the door and leave a bag of presents on the doorstep. In still other homes Sinterklaas and Zwarte Piet are hired to entertain and give out the presents during the family's St. Nicholas Eve celebration.

During the last half of the nineteenth century, only the urban middle and upper class celebrated St. Nicholas's Eve in this manner. In the countryside the children would put out their wooden shoes, filled with hay for Sinterklaas's horse, in anticipation of the saint leaving little goodies for them during the night.

During the twentieth century the adults also began exchanging gifts on St. Nicholas Eve. They would exchange little "surprises" as they would call their presents. The presents were sometimes disguised by wrapping a small present in a huge box. Along with the surprises, the gift givers would create poems, which would make fun of the habits, character, or recent events in the recipients' lives. Sometimes a treasure hunt for the gift would ensue. Eventually the children joined the practice and gave their parents gifts too.

Though the people of the Netherlands celebrate St. Nicholas Eve with great relish, Christmas day has never been as widely enjoyed. However, in the southern regions close to Germany and Belgium in the latter part of the twentieth century, De Kerstman (Father Christmas) has been known to bring presents on Christmas Eve.

De Kerstman
Vintage postcard
Postally used 1939

NORWAY

The roots of the Norwegian gift exchange on New Year's Day derive from the customs surrounding the Roman celebration of the kalends of January. During this festival the elite class gave presents to their servants as a reward for good service throughout the past year. Similarly, Norwegian kings were giving gifts to their subordinates as early as the eleventh century. In the fifteenth and sixteenth centuries, the gifts were mostly food related.

New Year's gift giving continued after the Middle Ages and carried into the nineteenth century. From the latter part of the sixteenth century there was evidence of Protestant children receiving Christmas gifts. By the eighteenth and twentieth centuries gift exchanges were practiced among equals.

During the Middle Ages, presents were exchanged by adults at Christmas as well as at the new year. Giving gifts to children was independent from the adult custom, and it began by associating the children with St. Nicholas and his feast day. Gifts to children in Norway did not become popular until the latter part of the nineteenth century, when the Julenisse became popular throughout Scandinavia.

The Norwegian nisse was very similar to the Swedish nisse. On Christmas Eve the Norwegians always left the nisse a bowl of rice porridge or pudding to pacify him and ensure a good year of plentiful crops and peaceful living. The Norwegian nisse was smaller in stature than the Swedish Julenisse. The nisse had a long beard and wore knee pants, wooden shoes, and a red stocking cap. The lore of the Julenisse and the original barn nisse merged in the twentieth century. On Christmas Eve they would knock at the door, open it, and yell in a strong voice, "Are there any good children living here?" If there was an affirmative answer (of course there always was), the Julenisse would bring in a bag of presents to distribute to the children.

Norwegian children, in recent times, write letters to a more American version of Santa Claus. He now lives in the Finnish Lapland rather than in Norway.

A Norwegian Nisse
Vintage postcard
Postally used 1918

POLAND

In Poland it wasn't until the first half of the eighteenth century that gift giving to children began. Swiety Mikolaj (St. Nicholas) came to Polish children on the eve of his feast day, December 6. He was accompanied by a devil-like figure or one or more angels. Swiety Mikolaj would question the children on their prayers and Bible lessons, awarding good responses with gifts, such as heart-shaped honey spice cakes called pierniki, toys, fruit, nuts, or winter clothing.

Throughout the last century Swiety Mikolaj, wearing bishop's clothing, would ride into a village in a horse-drawn sleigh. He often would have the children recite a prayer, particularly the Lord's Prayer. If they did not know the prayer, the children were the recipients of a lump of coal.

In other stories, Swiety Mikolaj would leave his gifts during the night, while the children were sleeping. Children would leave their polished boots for him to fill with gifts, or the saint would leave gifts under the children's pillows. When the children awoke and found their presents, their parents would remind them they should remember to thank Swiety Mikolaj in their prayers. In more recent times, when they celebrate St. Nicholas Day, children exchange gifts among each other at school.

Receiving gifts on Christmas Eve was first introduced in Poland in the twentieth century. Originally only children received small gifts, which the parents would hide around the homestead, either in the house or the barn. In time the children fused the image and folklore of St. Nicholas, sometimes called the Father of Christmas, and the American Santa.

In some regions of Poland, a little angel known as Aniolek, might have brought the gifts and put them under the tree on Christmas Eve. Her story probably originated with the angels that accompanied Swiety Mikolaj.

When the Communists were in power during

Swiety Mikolaj, vintage postcard
Printed in Poland, postally used ca. 1930

the last century, they introduced Grandfather Frost as their gift giver. He brought gifts on New Year's Day, for the followers of Communism did not recognize the Christian religion in their society. They referred to the Christian Christmas as the Family Day, Winter Holiday, or Little Star Day.

The name of Little Star Day relates to a Polish custom from the last century. The people of Poland would wait to begin the festivities until the first star shone in the evening sky on Christmas Eve. The first part of the celebration was a special Christmas Eve supper. At the end of the supper the children were led into another room. The Starman, sometimes referred to as "Little Star," arrived from Starland accompanied by the

Starboys. Dressed as Father Christmas, the Starman questioned the children on their catechism. He admonished those who answered incorrectly. The Starman then led the children back to the dining room, which was well decorated. His helpers had arranged the presents for the good children, but they would receive a birch switch if there was need for behavioral improvement.

Swiety Mikolaj, vintage postcard, postally used ca.1930

PORTUGAL

In the past century, O Pai Natal, or Father Christmas, visited the children of Portugal on Christmas Eve. The children would leave their shoes by the fireplace and would find small presents and sweets in them on Christmas day.

In the last fifty years, Santa Claus has brought the presents in some homes on Christmas Eve, while in others the baby Jesus brings the children their presents. But whoever the gift giver may be, the gifts are left under the Christmas tree on Christmas morning.

Many of Portugal's Christmas traditions have been influenced by Spain, which borders Portugal to the north and east. January 6, Epiphany, is very important in these areas. This is the time that the three Magi finally arrived to find the baby Jesus and present their gifts. On the eve of Epiphany, children put their shoes, filled with hay and carrots, on the window sills or by the doorways. The children hope that the wise men's horses (the Magi rode horses instead of camels in this area), will smell the food. As a result, the horses will bring the men to the children's homes, and the children will find presents in their shoes in the morning.

O Pai Natal
Vintage postcard
Postally used 1954

ROMANIA

In Romania the Christmas season begins on the eve of December 6, when St. Nicholas, or Mos Nicolae (Old Nicholas), as the Romanians have called him, arrives. He distributes presents to the good children and sometimes even to adults while they are sleeping. In anticipation of the saint's coming, the children and adults put a high polish on their boots or shoes, which they may leave on the window sill, as in early periods of Romanian culture, or at the main entrance, as is the more recent custom. The disobedient children receive what is called an "adorning rod," with which they are punished

During the Communist era, Grandfather Frost was the gift giver on New Year's Day. Since the fall of Communism, that custom has fallen out of practice. Christmas, of course, was frowned on by communist supporters, but they could not suppress the people's religious background. The Romanians continued to celebrate Christmas in the comforts of their homes.

Mos Craciun has been the most recent gift giver in Romania. He is much like the American Santa Claus and comes down the chimney on Christmas Eve. He either leaves his presents in stockings that the children hang in anticipation of his coming or places them under the Christmas tree.

Mos Nicolae
Vintage postcard
Postally used 1920

Mos Nicolae
Vintage postcard
ca. 1918

RUSSIA

In the eighteenth century, Germans migrated to Russia and formed colonies near the Volga River. Most of the settlers retained their German Christmas customs and called their gift givers by variants of the German names. These figures were Belznichol, the fur-clad St. Nicholas, and Kriskind, the Christ child.

Babouschka, an old, lovable Russian woman, brought the gifts to some of the Russian children in January. Her story was much like Befana of Italy. The three Magi had stopped by her house looking for the baby Jesus, but she told them that she was too busy cleaning her house to help them in their quest for the holy child. Later she changed her mind, but when she decided to join the wise men, she was unable to find them. Every year after that, she has sought the baby Jesus so that she could lead the three men to him. At every house she entered during her search, she left presents for the children.

Ded Moroz (Grandfather Frost or Father Frost) came into being during the time of the czars. At this time he lived far in the forests of Russia. He would come into the villages in a sleigh, called a *troika*, sometimes drawn by three horses. He brought presents door to door to the obedient youths after they were in bed; the naughty ones were ignored.

Then, in 1917, the Revolution against Czar Nicholas II brought about the end of the czars and the rise of Communism. The Communists suppressed Christianity and replaced the celebration of Christmas. To take the place of Christmas, they introduced the Russian people to the Winter Festival, and New Year's Day as their day of celebration. However, they retained Grandfather Frost as the gift giver for the children. He was accompanied by his granddaughter Snegurochka, the Snow Maiden, who was made of snow and ice.

Though the Communist reign has come to an end New Year's Day is still the most important holiday in Russia. Religious celebrations, including Christmas, are now tolerated. In the Russian Orthodox Church, Sviatki, the Christmas season, lasts from January 7 to January 19.

Ded Moroz
Vintage postcard
Postally used ca. 1910

Съ Рождествомъ
Христовымъ

Ded Moroz
Vintage postcard
Postally used 1915

Grandfather Frost and the Snow Maiden
Vintage postcard
ca. 1930

SPAIN

The gift givers of Spain, the Magi, have always come on January 5, the eve of Epiphany. In Spain the three men were seen everywhere during the Christmas season. They came by boat or on horseback, or by whatever means was available in the different regions of the country. Usually arriving on a donkey and bringing gifts, Balthazar has been the most popular of the wise men among the children of Spain.

On Epiphany Eve, the children of Spain would traditionally put out their shoes, filled with grain, straw, or other food for the animals that the wise men rode. During the night, the Magi, on their way to Bethlehem would leave presents for the children in and around the shoes.

The three Magi, vintage postcard, postally used 1945

SWEDEN

The festivities of the Christmas season in Sweden have started on St. Lucia's Day, the thirteenth of December, since the eleventh century. St. Lucia was a fourth century Sicilian Saint who Swedes have revered for reasons unknown. Some children put their shoes out on the eve of St. Lucia's Day for the little presents she might leave them. Sometimes she was accompanied by the Star Boys, carrying a star and dressed as three kings. The Star Boys had performed plays at Epiphany in earlier centuries and traveled in processions, singing songs and making merry.

In Sweden, there was no gift giver associated with Christmas Day before the mid-eighteenth century. Before that time, gift exchanging was associated with New Year's Day. From the mid-eighteenth century to the mid-nineteenth century, a Christmas goat called the Julbock was the bringer of gifts. Usually a relative dressed in skins and wore a goat head or mask to impersonate the Julbock, just as Americans often dress in Santa Claus suits to deliver presents. The tradition of the goat was adapted from Norse mythology and legends in which the god Thor traveled through his domain in a chariot driven by a pair of goats.

Another Christmas tradition emerged around the 1870s when Viktor Rydberg wrote a book entitled *Little Vigg's Christmas Eve*. With this book and its illustrations by painter and illustrator, Jenny Nystrom of Sweden, the "Jultomten," Christmas gnomes, came into being. The tales of goblins, or *tomten,* as they were called, were centuries old, but they had not been connected with Christmas until the publication of Rydberg's book.

Tomte came from the word *tomt,* meaning the ground under the house and the surrounding yard, because the tomte lived in the barn or under the floorboards in the house. Not always kind creatures, they were on the farm to oversee the proper treatment of the animals. If the animals were mistreated, a tomte would release mayhem on the family and farm. To appease the tomte, the farm family would ensure that the goblin-like creatures were not hungry. The farmer's wife would leave the tomte a meal of porridge and milk on Christmas Eve. The farmers and their families would have to be nice to the tomte if they wanted to have a good and prosperous year.

The tomten did not originally bring presents on Christmas or at any other time of the year. After Rydberg's book, however, the Jultomten became Christmas gift givers. The Jultomten would arrive after the Christmas Eve feast with a knock on the door and the question "Are there any good children here?" Then they would distribute gifts if the children were good.

Julbock, vintage postcard, postally used 1906

SWITZERLAND

The ways of celebrating the Christmas holiday season in Switzerland have varied according to the four different lingual regions. The celebrations are so diverse that they may even vary from one village to another.

In the Swiss-German Catholic areas, Samichlaus (otherwise known as St. Nicolas) arrived on the eve of St. Nicolas's feast day. He was usually accompanied by a donkey and at least one of his assistant Schmutzlis. The faces of the Schmutzlis were darkened with soot, and they were dressed in dark clothing.

When Samichlaus arrived at a home, he questioned the children on their Bible knowledge and prayers and their good and bad deeds. The Schmutzlis handed out nuts, fruit, and sweets or small gifts to the good children. In the early twentieth century there was a rod for the ill-behaved children. The Schmutzlis would even threaten to carry the children into the woods and "guzzle" them up.

The Christ child, vintage postcard, ca. 1912

In the German-speaking Protestant areas of Switzerland, the Christkindl brought the Christmas presents on Christmas Eve. In this part of the world, the Christ child was represented by a young female angel dressed in a white gown and wearing a shining crown on her head. As in Germany, she was sometimes accompanied by a dark figure similar to Knecht Ruprecht. Other times Christkindl was accompanied by angel helpers, and the ringing of a bell announced her arrival.

In some areas in the French-speaking regions of Switzerland, the gift giver was Le Petit Jesus (the baby Jesus). The children would pray to baby Jesus to bring them certain presents on the sixth of January. This day, of course, was when the Magi brought the baby Jesus their presents of gold, frankincense, and myrrh.

In other French-speaking areas, children received gifts on St. Nicolas Eve. When St. Nicolas brought his gifts, he would be accompanied by Pére Fouettard, as in France.

Samiclaus and the Schmutzlis
Vintage postcard, ca. 1920

SANTA IN AMERICA

If there is one person responsible for bringing Santa Claus to America, the credit should be given to Washington Irving, the author of *Rip Van Winkle*. He established the fame of Santa Claus by including this figure in his 1809 satirical account about the origins of the state of New York. Written under the pseudonym Diedrich Knickerbocker, Irving's work was titled *A History of New York from the Beginning of the World to the End of the Dutch Dynasty*. In the satire Irving mentioned St. Nicholas at least twenty-four times. This book intrigued the population, and Santa Claus began his journey into the history of America.

In Irving's book, he described a figurehead of St. Nicholas on one of the first Dutch ships to come to America as having a "low broad brimmed hat,

Santa Claus Paying His Usual Christmas Visit to His Young Friends in the United States
from Harper's Weekly, *December 25, 1858*

huge pair of Flemish trunk hose and a pipe that reached to the end of the bowsprit." This was a very different image from our present-day Santa, but Irving also provided a characterization of Santa Claus that remains familiar today. Irving mentioned in his book that St. Nicholas rode over the rooftops and trees in his horse-drawn wagon, delivering presents to the children. Other familiar descriptions of the American gift giver that can be found in Irving's book include the way " the smoke from his pipe encircled over head" and his famous mannerism of "laying his finger beside his nose." Irving also mentioned that "when St. Nicholas had smoked his pipe he twisted it in his hat band"

and after delivering his presents "he mounted his wagon and disappeared over the tree top."

James K. Paulding, a friend of Washington Irving, was the author of *Origin of the Baker's Dozen* in which he contributed to Irving's portrayal and described St. Nicholas as "a little rascal with a three-cornered cocked hat, decked with gold lace, a blue Dutch sort of short pea jacket, red waistcoat, breeks [breeches] of the same color, yellow stockings and honest thick soled shoes, ornamented with a pair of skates."

Though Irving is responsible for popularizing Santa Claus, we can not forget the immigrants from Germany and other countries who also contributed

Santa Claus *from* Harper's Weekly, *December 28, 1867*

Vintage postcard marked PFB Serie 9593
Printed in Germany, postally used 1909

the nineteenth century, as early as 1769 there is mention that German settlers observed Christmas in church services. Despite the reemergence of Christmas, there were die-hard "Knickerbockers," descendants of elite immigrants to old New York, who continued to glorify the new year with gift giving into the 1880s. However, other inhabitants of New York City began celebrating Christmas as the main holiday around 1820.

The origin of the name "Santa Claus" evolved over a fairly short period of time from the late eighteenth century into the nineteenth century. It has quite often been attributed to a transformation of the Dutch word "Sinterklaas," which meant St. Nicholas. But in America, Santa Claus was first called St. Claus, St. A. Claus, or Sanct Claus. Sanct Claus meant "Holy Man Nicholas." Several of Germany's gift givers had the name of Klaus or Klas as a part of their name, which has been referred to as a deviation of the name Nicholas, so it was a natural evolution to the name Santa Claus.

The German immigrants in America, many of whom settled in Pennsylvania, brought their Christmas customs. According to a newspaper article in the December 30, 1887, *Daily Examiner* of Lancaster, Pennsylvania, the Rev. A. W. Kauffman gave the following account of one Christmas Eve to a group of adults and children at Sunday service.

The reverend referred to Christmas Eve in 1822, when he was only seven years old and worked as a hired hand for an old farmer. The farmer told him to set out his basket as the old Kris Kingle (a derivative of the German Christkindl or Christ child) would come that night. He did as he was told, but instead of a large plate or beautiful basket, he was given a large straw breadbasket. The reverend was also informed that he must put hay in the basket for Kris Kingle's mule. He told the audience that the Kris Kingle was not as high-toned as Santa had become by 1887. Instead of a fine team of reindeer and a beautiful sleigh and

All Good Wishes for Christmas.

to his presence in America. Christmas was not celebrated in the colonies during the seventeenth and eighteenth centuries. In fact, the Puritans fined people who participated in such festivities. Christmas, according to the Puritans, was to be a regular workday, for they believed the celebration had pagan roots and had become too rowdy in England. The populace then geared their wintertime merrymaking toward New Year's Day, which became a family holiday. There was an exchange of gifts on this day, but no gift giver in early America.

While many people still celebrated New Year's Day as the big winter holiday into the early half of bells, he came on an old gray mule. The reverend went on to say that he found walnuts, snits, choostets, and starched gingerbread in his basket the next morning.

This "setting of a basket" lasted well into the nineteenth century. The gifts of the Christkindel became known as the "Christ Kindly," coming to mean the same as what we call Christmas presents. When the Pennsylvania Dutch, of German origin, intermarried with the English residents, Christkindel evolved into Kriss Kringle. This then became, along with Santa Claus and St. Nicholas, a name for America's gift giver.

Some of the German immigrants had brought along another gift giver, Pelznichol. There were numerous spelling variations of this name, which meant fur-clad St. Nicholas. Pelznichol brought the presents of Christmas, but he also brought switches or rods and scared the children with the notion that he would carry them away in his bag if they misbehaved. In Germany he had sometimes accompanied the Christ child, but in America he came alone, sometimes on a donkey as he did in Germany.

Another description of a Santa Claus, which Penne L. Restad mentions in her book *Christmas in America*, was in an article of the *New York Herald*. It stated, "When Santa visited a New York ball one Christmas Eve, he appeared clad in large buckskin boots, dark brown coat, fawn-colored pants with a blue stripe, and a red vest with big brass buttons that 'encircled a truly aldermanic

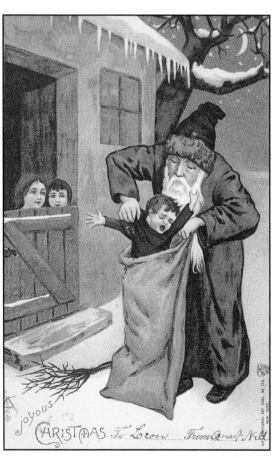

Vintage postcard, International Art Publ. Co. ca. 1910

Pelznichol from Our Holidays Retold *from* St. Nicholas, *1905*

paunch.' An 'ample cloak of scarlet and gold' completed his attire."

Of course the most famous description of Santa Claus can be found in Clement C. Moore's poem, *An Account of a Visit of St. Nicholas*, which came to be known as *'Twas the Night Before Christmas*. There are various accounts of how Moore was inspired to

write his classic poem. One version has it that in 1822 Moore's daughter Charity asked her father to write a poem for Christmas. With his daughter's request in mind, Moore started thinking of his friend Irving's descriptions of St. Nicholas in his history of New York. It is also thought that Moore had read another book published in 1821 entitled *A New*

ON THE CHIMNEY TOP.

On the Chimney Top, *Illustration from* The Night Before Christmas, *ca. 1890s*

Year's Present to the Little Ones from Five to Twelve. In this book, "Santeclaus," as the author called the gift giver in his poem, was pictured in a sleigh pulled by one reindeer. This was the first illustration of a reindeer pulling Santa's sleigh as well as the first time Santa was depicted in a red suit.

Inspired, Moore created the poem on his way to get a turkey for Christmas dinner, while riding in his sleigh driven by his jolly and plump yardman. When he arrived home, he wrote the poem down, and his family loved it. The poem was first published in the *Sentinel* of Troy, New York in 1823, but Moore did not admit to authoring the poem until 1837. Though it is Moore's image of a merry Christmas visitor that has shaped our perception of the American gift giver, Santa Claus continued to be described and illustrated in a variety of ways through the last half of the nineteenth century.

One aspect of the Santa Claus lore that emerged after Moore's poem was published was the Christmas elf. Elves sprinted onto the scene to help Santa around the 1850s. "The Wonders of Santa Claus," a poem illustrated in the December 26, 1857, issue of *Harper's Weekly*, was one of the

Book Cover, A Visit of St. Nicholas
McLoughlin Bros., NY, 1896

first times that elves were mentioned in connection with Christmas. Though Louisa May Alcott had written a collection of fairy stories in 1855 called "The Christmas Elves," *Harper's* rejected it, and it went unpublished. During the latter part of the nineteenth century, Santa's helpers were referred to as fairies, elves, or brownies.

Then along came Thomas Nast, a great political cartoonist for *Harper's Weekly* in the last half of the nineteenth century. An important contributor to the evolution of the image of Santa Claus in America, Nast was also the political cartoonist responsible for creating the elephant for the Republican Party and the donkey for the Democrats. Nast drew his first cartoon for *Harper's Weekly* in 1859 and his last in 1896. During this period, Nast drew many illustrations of Santa for *Harper's Weekly*. He drew his first illustration of Santa at the beginning of the Civil War. Featured on the cover of the January 3, 1863, *Harper's*

Vintage postcard, German-American Novelty Series 628, printed in Germany Postally used 1906

Assistant to Santa Claus from The Graphic *Christmas Number 1914*

Weekly, Santa was dressed in a patriotic uniform of stars and stripes while he delivered presents to the Civil War soldiers. Another drawing depicted Santa in an all-fur suit, probably influenced from the version of Pelznichol in Nast's country of birth, Germany.

Nast also played a part in introducing Santa to another familiar, though not particularly seasonal, character that entered the Christmas scene in the last part of the nineteenth century: Mother Goose. Thomas Nast's prominent cartoon of Mother Goose and Santa dancing together appeared on the cover of *Harper's Weekly* on January 3, 1880. Santa also appeared with Mother Goose in children's books of this era.

The strong national interest in Santa Claus, which was represented by the popularity of Nast's illustrations, led to the development of additional stories about the Christmas figure. It seems to have been in the 1880s when Mrs. Santa Claus

Thomas Nast illustration from Harper's Weekly *January 3, 1863*

came into Santa's domain. It made sense; Santa needed someone to take care of him and manage the elves.

The first reference to a wife for Santa or St. Nicholas was in an article, "A Glimpse of an Old Dutch Town," in the March 1881 issue of *Harper's New Monthly* magazine. Referring to seventeenth-century practices in the town of Albany, New York, the article stated, "Christmas was of little importance among the Dutch, for New Year was *the* day, and then it was that the right fat, jolly, roistering little St. Nicholas made his appearance, sometimes accompanied by his good-natured vrouw [wife], Molly Grietje." The article was not a factual story about the early Dutch settlers. In reality, the immigrants to that area were mostly Protestant Walloons and Huguenots and were not of the Catholic religion to which St. Nicholas belonged.

In the December 1884 issue of *St. Nicholas* magazine, a poem, "Visiting Santa Claus" by Lucy Larcom, includes Santa's wife putting on her spectacles and looking over Santa's shoulder. In the December 1885 issue of *St. Nicholas* magazine, another poem entitled "Mrs. Kriss Kringle" by Edith M. Thomas is devoted to Mrs. Claus. In the poem Thomas describes her as a "Dear old lady, small and rosy!"

Thomas Nast illustration from Harper's Weekly *January 3, 1880*

Katharine Lee Bates, the author of "America the Beautiful," also wrote a poem about Mr. and Mrs. Santa Claus entitled "Goody Santa Claus on a Sleigh-Ride." It was published in the *Wide Awake* periodical in December 1888.

During this period (the end of the nineteenth century and the beginning of the twentieth century) Santa's popularity could be measured in the mail he received. How else could he have known what the nation's children wanted for Christmas? Santa could not be everywhere at once. The mail situation was first seen in book illustrations in the late 1880s.

The popularity of Santa continued to grow. Even international events could not subdue America's love of Santa Claus. During World War I, Santa was not forgotten. He joined the army. A

Illustration of "Goody Santa Claus on a Sleigh-Ride" from Wide Awake, *December 1888*

well-known artist of the day, J. C. Leyendecker, portrayed Santa in army garb with a Christmas tree and a massive book, which listed good and bad children, tucked under his arm. With his army helmet on, Santa saluted the young men of the service. Leyendecker sold his first cover to the *Saturday Evening Post* in 1889. He went on to paint over three hundred covers for the *Post*.

Another of Leyendecker's Santa illustrations on the cover of the *Saturday Evening Post* for December 7, 1912, depicted a Salvation Army Santa ringing bells and collecting money for the poor. In 1937 the Salvation Army terminated its custom of using locals for impersonating Santa at their collection points. They had received too many complaints that it confused and disillusioned children.

Magazine cover by J. C. Leyendecker from Saturday Evening Post *December 7, 1918*

However, one custom that preserved the wonder of the holiday season was the tradition of exchanging holiday cards. The "Golden Age of Postcards" emerged between 1898 and 1918. Everyone, adults and children alike, collected the beautiful lithographic cards. Christmas postcards were a large portion of those collections, just as they are today, and many scrapbooks were filled with the handsome images. Germany produced the more sought-after postcards. The colors were rich and striking, and the varieties of cards were spectacular. Of course, Germany produced Santa postcards that depicted the gift givers of Europe rather than the American Santa. However, that did not deter the American people from mailing and giving the postcards, which sold for a price of two to five cents, to friends, family, and neighbors.

Hundreds of thousands of Christmas and Santa postcards were generated during the "Golden Age of Postcards," and the creative minds behind the cards had to constantly generate ideas to keep up with the demand for new images. To reinvent the popular subject on the postcards, Santas were shown wearing robes of different colors or patterns. The most collectible today are colors other than the traditional red. Of course, Santas were pictured with children, for they were the central purpose behind Santa's

Vintage postcard marked PFB, ca. 1906

role as gift giver. Postcards showing Santa full length were also desirable. Full-length views showed off the costume of Santa much more than a small figure in a large landscape. Santa was even portrayed delivering his presents in new modes of transportation—animals, bicycles, motor cars, trains, and sleighs drawn by animals other than reindeer.

Capturing the great variety inherent in the depictions of Santa, the December 26, 1857, issue of *Harper's Weekly* included an excerpt from the lengthy poem "The Wonders of Santa Claus," which described the scene of Santa's departure on Christmas Eve.

December's four and twentieth day
Through its course was almost run,
St. Nicholas stood at his castle door
Awaiting the setting sun.
His goods were packed in a great balloon,
Near by were his horse and sleigh:
He had his skates upon his feet
And a ship getting under weigh.

Despite the earlier discrepancies in the portrayals of the famous Christmas gift giver, the image of Santa by the 1920s and 1930s was well established. The era of the beautiful postcards had also come to an end, but Santa lived on.

Vintage postcard, printed in Germany
Postally used 1908

Vintage postcard, printed in Germany
ca. 1910

Illustration from "Christmas Boxes," McLoughlin Bros., NY, ca. 1890s

Book Cover, A Visit of St. Nicholas, McLoughlin Bros., NY, 1896

Illustration of Mother Goose and Santa from Mother Goose's Ball
Lothrop Co., Boston, ca. 1890s

CHRISTMAS STOCKING NUMBER

VOL. XLI, No. 2   DECEMBER, 1913   PRICE, 25 CENTS

ST. NICHOLAS
ILLUSTRATED MAGAZINE
FOR BOYS AND GIRLS

FREDERICK WARNE & CO . BEDFORD ST · STRAND · LONDON
THE · CENTURY · CO · UNION · SQUARE · NEW · YORK

Magazine cover
St. Nicholas
December 1913

*Thomas Nast illustration
from* Harper's Weekly
December 12, 1882

Pioneer Santa, *Cover of* Harper's Weekly
January 2, 1869

Magazine cover by J. C. Leyendecker
from Saturday Evening Post
December 7, 1912

*Vintage postcard
Marked B. W. 198
Printed in Germany
Postally used 1907*

*Vintage postcard
Marked S L & Co. N1319
Printed in Germany
Postally Used 1908*

*Vintage postcard
ca. 1908*

*Vintage postcard, signed "Clapsaddle"
Printed in Germany, ca. 1910*

*Vintage postcard, printed in Germany
Postally used 1909*

Vintage postcard, printed in
Germany, postally used 1910

Vintage postcard, printed in
Germany, ca. 1910

Vintage postcard, APM Co.
Santa Claus Series 404, ca. 1910

Vintage postcard, printed in
Germany, postally used 1909

Saint Nicholas reading his mail
Illustration from unknown book, 1889

Inspecting the Toys
unknown origin, 1901

Vintage postcard
ca. 1910

Vintage postcard
Printed in Saxony
Postally used 1908

Vintage postcard marked JBC
Christmas Series No. 555
ca. 1910

Vintage postcard, printed in Germany, postally used ca. 1910

Vintage postcard, postally used 1936

RESOURCES AND FURTHER READING GUIDE

Imagery of vintage Christmas postcards, greeting cards, trade cards, die cuts, book and newspaper illustrations, and engravings from 1846 to approximately 1954 from the author's Christmas collection. All photography of imagery is by the author.

BOOKS AND PERIODICALS

Bates, Katharine Lee, "Goody Santa Claus on a Sleigh-Ride," *Wide Awake Periodical* Vol. 28 (December 1888).

Bowler, Gerry. *The World Encyclopedia of Christmas*. Toronto: McClelland and Steward, 2000.

Crippen, T. G. *Christmas and Christmas Lore*. 1928. Reprint, Detroit: Omnigraphics, 1990.

DeRobeck, Nester. *The Christmas Crib*. Milwaukee: The Bruce Publishing Co., 1956.

Foley, Daniel J. *The Christmas Tree: An Evergreen Garland Filled with History, Folklore, Symbolism, Traditions, Legends and Stories*. Philadelphia and New York: Chilton Co., 1960.

Gardiner, Horace J. *Let's Celebrate Christmas*. New York: A. S. Barnes & Co., 1940.

Guerber, H. A. *Myths of Northern Lands*. New York: American Book Co., 1895.

Hart, Cynthia, John Grossman, and Priscilla Dunhill. *Joy to the World: A Victorian Christmas*. New York: Workman Publishing Co., 1990.

Henriksen, Vera. *Christmas in Norway Past and Present*. Norway: Tanum-Norli, 1981.

Hervey, Thomas K. *The Book of Christmas*. Boston: Roberts Brothers, 1888.

Hole, Christina. *English Custom and Usage*. 2d ed. London: B. T. Batsford Publishers, 1943-44.

Hottes, Alfred Carl. *1001 Christmas Facts and Fancies*. New York: A. T. DeLaMare Co., 1937.

Vintage postcard, International Art Publ. Co. Series No. 1197, printed in Germany, ca. 1910

The Life and Times of St. Francis. Trans. Arnoldo Mondadori. Curtis International Portraits of Greatness. Italy: The Curtis Publishing Co. and Arnoldo Mondadori, 1965.

Miles, Clement A. *Christmas in Ritual and Tradition, Christian and Pagan.* 1912. Reprint, *Christmas Customs and Traditions, Their History and Significance.* New York: Dover Publications, 1976.

Polanie Club Inc. *Treasured Polish Christmas Customs and Traditions.* Minneapolis: Polanie Publishing Co., 1972.

Restad, Penne L. *Christmas in America: A History.* New York: Oxford University Press, 1995.

Ruland, Jose. *Christmas in Germany.* Trans. Timothy Nevill, Charlton. Bonn, Germany: Hohwacht Verlag in collaboration with Inter Nationes Bonn-Bad Godesberg, 1978.

Sandys, William. *Christmastide, Its History, Festivities and Carols.* London: John Russell Smith Publishers, n.d.

Segall, Barbara. *The Christmas Tree.* New York: Clarkson Potter Publishers, 1995.

Vintage postcard
Printed in Germany
Postally used 1918

Siefker, Phyllis. *Santa Claus: Last of the Wild Men.* Jefferson, NC: McFarland and Co. Publishers, 1997.

Snyder, Phillip V. *The Christmas Tree Book.* New York: Viking Press, 1976.

Vintage postcard
International Art Publ. Co.
Series No. 1649
Printed in Germany
Postally used, ca 1910

Stephenson, Michael. *The Christmas Almanac.* Oxford: Oxford University Press, 1992.

Stevens, Patricia Bunning. *Merry Christmas—A History of the Holiday.* New York: MacMillan Publishing Co., 1979.

Stokker, Kathleen. *Keeping Christmas Yuletide Traditions in Norway and the New Land.* St. Paul, Minnesota: Historical Society Press, 2000.

Swedish Christmas. Compiled and issued by Ewert Cagner in cooperation with Dr. Goran Axel-Nilsson and Dr. Henrik Sandblad. Gothenburg, Sweden: Tre Tryckare, 1955.

Thonger, Richard. *A Calendar of German Customs.* London: Oswald Wolff Publishers, 1966.

Walsh, William S. *Curiosities of Popular Customs and of Rites, Ceremonies, Observances and Miscellaneous Antiquities.* Philadelphia: J. B. Lippincott, 1898.

Warren, Nathan B. *The Holidays: Christmas, Easter, Whitsuntide.* New York: Hurd and Houghton, 1868.

Harrison, Michael. *The Story of Christmas.* London: Odhams Press, n.d.

Irving, Washington. *Knickerbocker's History of New York.* N.p.: A.L. Burt Company, n.d.

Jones, Charles W. *Saint Nicholas of Myra, Bari and Manhattan: Biography of a Legend.* Chicago: The University of Chicago Press, 1978.

Marling, Karal Ann. *Merry Christmas: Celebrating America's Greatest Holiday.* Cambridge, MA: Howard University Press, 2000.

Matthews, John. *The Winter Solstice: The Sacred Traditions of Christmas.* Wheaton, IL: Godsfield Press and Qwest Books, Theosophical Publishing House, 1998.

Sansom, William. *A Book of Christmas.* New York: McGraw-Hill, 1968.

Shoemaker, Alfred L. *Christmas in Pennsylvania.* Originally published in 1959 by the Pennsylvania Folklife Society.

Tanya, Gulevich. *Encyclopedia of Christmas.* Omnigraphics, 2000.

BOOKS FOR FURTHER READING

Buday, George. *The History of the Christmas Card.* London: Spring Books, 1964.

Chris, Teresa. *The Story of Santa Claus.* New Jersey: Chartwell Books, Quintet Publishing, 1992.

Coffin, Tristram Potter. *The Illustrated Book of Christmas Folklore.* New York: The Seabury Press, 1973.

Connelly, Mark. *Christmas: A Social History.* London: I. B. Tauris Publishers, 1999.

De Groot, Adriaan D. *Saint Nicholas: A Psychoanalytic Study of His History & Myth.* Paris: Mouton & Company, 1965.

Ebon, Martin. *Saint Nicholas: Life and Legend.* New York: Harper & Row, 1975.

Foley, Daniel J. *Christmas the World Over.* Philadelphia: Chilton Books Publishers, 1963.

Vintage postcard, ca. 1910